T0358720

ISLAMIC STATES IN JAVA
1500—1700

VERHANDELINGEN

VAN HET KONINKLIJK INSTITUUT
VOOR TAAL-, LAND- EN VOLKENKUNDE

70

ISLAMIC STATES IN JAVA
1500-1700

EIGHT DUTCH BOOKS AND ARTICLES BY Dr H. J. DE GRAAF

as summarized by

THEODORE G. Th. PIGEAUD

with a Comprehensive List of Sources
and a General Index of Names

composed by

H. J. DE GRAAF

THE HAGUE - MARTINUS NIJHOFF 1976

I.S.B.N. 90.247.1876.7

PREFACE

The growing interest in the history of Indonesia has made it desirable to have an English summary of the principal works of the Dutch historian Dr H. J. de Graaf, who in several books and articles published between 1935 and 1973 has given a description of the development of the Javanese kingdom of Mataram, based both on European and indigenous material. His works form a substantial contribution to the study of the national history of Indonesia.

The Summary contains references to the paragraphs of the Dutch books and articles. This makes it easy for those readers who have a knowledge of Dutch to consult the original texts. The List of Sources for the study of Javanese history from 1500 to 1700 is composed of the lists in the summarized books and articles, and the Index of Names refers not only to the present Summary but also to the eight original texts. Many names of persons and localities in the Index have been provided with short explanatory notes and references to other *lemmata* as a quick way to give some provisional information on Javanese history. The spelling of all Javanese words and names has been modernized in accordance with the rules of orthography of Indonesian languages which have been laid down by Government. (Only the scholarly ḍ, ṭ and ĕ have been retained where it seemed convenient to do so.)

Dr M. C. Ricklefs, of the School of Oriental and African Studies, London, has taken the trouble to correct the English of the Summary. He may rest assured that his helpfulness is greatly appreciated.

TABLE OF CONTENTS

I.

THE FIRST ISLAMIC STATES OF JAVA
15th AND 16th CENTURIES

Summary of:

H. J. de Graaf en Th. G. Th. Pigeaud, De eerste moslimse
vorstendommen op Java. Studiën over de staatkundige geschiedenis van de 15de en 16de eeuw. 's-Gravenhage 1974.
*Verhandelingen van het Koninklijk Instituut voor Taal-,
Land- en Volkenkunde.* Vol. 69.

I. THE FIRST ISLAMIC STATES

Introduction, 1. Historiography of Java

p. 7. The political independence from foreign powers, which was won after world-war II, aroused in Indonesia a desire for a national history which should describe past developments from an Indonesian point of view and be based chiefly on indigenous material. The history of pre-Islamic Java written by professor Krom of Leiden seemed to come up to the requirements. It was accepted as a beginning for the wished-for national history. Books on the Islamic period written by European authors were found less satisfactory because they were based chiefly on material supplied by foreigners. Indigenous sources of information were neglected by European authors because they were considered unreliable.

The existing books on the Islamic period of Javanese history require reconsideration and supplementing on the following four points. The idea that the decline and fall of the Shiwaitic-Buddhistic dynasty of Majapahit in the first quarter of the 16th century and the coming into power of the Islamic rulers of Děmak meant the end of an old civilization and the beginning of a completely new, Islamic one must be reconsidered. It is far more likely that Islamization proceeded slowly, and it is certain that numerous elements of pre-Islamic culture survived in the succeeding period.

A second matter which requires attention is the tendency to over-emphasize the role of the ruling dynasty of Mataram. Events and developments outside the royal residence and among the common people in the villages are too much neglected in the books on history.

A third area of the history of Java which must be supplemented by new studies is the development of local and national economies during the past six or seven centuries. What was written on this subject by European authors was based on information supplied by foreign sea-farers and traders who were chiefly interested in the production of the goods they bought and sold. The economy of the villages in the interior of the country was beyond their ken.

The fourth aspect of Javanese history which is unduly neglected is the development and composition of the population. From prehistoric times to the twentieth century a great number of migrations by Javanese,

Sundanese, Madurese and Balinese people from one area of the islands to another must have taken place. Moreover, the fertile and prosperous coastal provinces attracted foreign adventurers and traders who in many cases became settlers.

The foreign settlements which contributed most to the development of Javanese culture were in the first place Indian, and then Indo-Chinese. Indian civilization had a lasting influence in the fields of literature and religion in the pre-Islamic period. In accordance with Javanese popular tradition, it can now be stated that Indo-Chinese traders took a great part in the spreading of Islam in East and Central Java. The European colonization, lastly, is responsible for improvements in land and sea communication, economic expansion and public health measures, which allowed a vast increase of the population in the past two centuries.

Introduction, 2. History of Java in the 15th and 16th centuries

p. 11. The knowledge of pre-Islamic history benefited greatly from the energy spent by the archeologists on the remains of Old Javanese temples. If in the future as much energy and money are spent on archeological excavations on Islamic sites, knowledge of the history of many places mentioned in the following pages woud vastly increase.

There are several points made in the present discussion of the beginning of the Islamic period. Firstly, Islam became dominant in Java by degrees. Islamic middle-class people of mixed blood who were residents of long standing in the North Coast harbour towns, took over control of their districts from the local rulers, who were high-born men and vassals of the Shiwaitic-Buddhistic King of Majapahit. They acknowledged the King as their liege lord, however, and continued in secular matters in the way of their "heathen" predecessors. The next development was the attack by a group of Muslim fanatics from Central Java on the royal residence of Majapahit, which led to the fall of the Shiwaitic-Buddhistic dynasty, probably in 1527. The local ruler of Děmak, a man of partly Chinese extraction, took advantage of the opportunity to extend his authority over most of the other districts of the realm, and to take the Islamic title of Sultan.

After his death in the middle of the 16th century a period of confusion followed. This ended when the rulers of Mataram, at that time a little-cultivated district in the interior of the country, took over control in Central Java and extended their authority in East Java as far as Surabaya by conquest. The move of the political and cultural centre of Java from Děmak and Surabaya, harbour towns on the North Coast with a mixed population, into the interior of the country was of great consequence. In the more than three centuries during which kings of the House of Mataram were able to reign under the protection of Dutch power, a Javanese national feeling had time to develop. The civilization of the Mataram Court, which flourished in the 18th and 19th centuries, was an important factor for cultural unity. At present, it is still a source of inspiration for the development of a common Indonesian civilization.

*Introduction, 3. Sources of information on Javanese history of the
16th and 17th centuries*

p. 14. The sources which are used in the present book are: (1) the "Relacion" of the Portuguese traveller Tomé Pires, a contemporary who left Java in 1515. (2) The Javanese books on history called Sĕrat Kaṇḍa (Books of Tales) and Babad Mataram (Dynastic History of the House of Mataram). The Books of Tales contain descriptions of the Dĕmak period of history, based on nearly contemporary information. They were, in an abridged form, included in the Mataram History, which was written in the 18th century. (3) Local histories of regional dynasties who were vanquished by the Mataram forces in the 17th century. (4) Lists of memorable years, called Babad Sangkala. Some of them contain information on events which were not mentioned in the elaborate Books of Tales or Dynastic Histories. (5) Genealogies of royal and noble families. Although the beginning of many pedigrees is legendary or even mythic, the later parts often contain reliable and interesting information. (6) Legends of the Saints who are believed to have been the first preachers of Islam in Java. Although miracles take an important place in these legends, they deserve the attention of historians because they provide information on the Muslim middle class of traders to which many Saints originally belonged. (7) Chinese notes referring to the Indo-Chinese trading settlements in the coastal provinces of Java. Memorials found in the Chinese imperial archives are among the most important sources of information on the pre-Islamic history of Java. An Indonesian book by Parlindungan, published not long ago, contains a chapter on the beginning of Islam in Java which may be based upon genuine Chinese notes on history. As long as the origin of Parlindungan's information is not known, however, it seems best to omit references to his book.

Chpt. 1. *The beginning of Islam in Java*

§ *1.* East Javanese legends refer to Islamic holy men in the 15th century. Cĕmpa (Champa) is said to have been the native country of the first Muslims who came to Java, the Princess (Putri Cĕmpa) who married the still-"Buddhistic" King of Majapahit (Bra Wijaya), and her two nephews, the sons of an "Arabic" man of religion. The elder nephew is said to have been imām of the mosque of Grĕsik and the younger one is known as radèn Rahmat of Ngampèl Dĕnta, a quarter of the town of Surabaya where he lived and was buried (2nd half of the 15th cent.). He was the ancestor of a long line of Muslim men of religion, and the most senior of the nine saints (Wali Sanga) who, according to 17th century Javanese tradition, spread the Faith in East and Central Java. Dates on Islamic tombstones found in various places in East Java testify, however, to the presence of Muslim communities of some importance in the pre-Islamic Javanese kingdoms as early as the 12th century. According to a recently published, but not wholly trustworthy Chinese tradition perhaps deriving from some ancient Sino-Javanese trading centres in Central and West Java, the famous Muslim admiral Cheng Ho was the founder of several Chinese Islamic communities on the North Coast in the beginning of the 15th century.

§ 2. In all probability the Cĕmpa of Javanese tradition, the native country of radèn Rahmat of Ngampèl Dĕnta, is to be identified with the ancient state of Champa in what is now South Vietnam, which was finally overrun by Vietnamese conquerors in the third quarter of the 15th century. The royal family supposedly fled and was converted to Islam at the Court of Sultan Mansur Shah of Malaka (1458-1477). It is possible that the small port of Jeumpa on the North coast of Acheh may have had some connection with Champa.

§ 3. The economy of the Majapahit kingdom in the interior of East Java was based on agriculture, especially rice cultivation. Trading communities of mixed Javanese and foreign (especially Indian and Chinese), descent had existed in several harbour towns on the North Coast for many centuries, offering facilities as intermediate stations on the international trade route from India and China to the Spice Islands. Some commercial centres on the North Coast of Java also had ocean-going ships of their own, fitted out for trade to India, the Malay Peninsula, China, the Philippines and the countries between.

§ 4. From the tenth century onward members of mixed-descent trading communities in South-East Asian harbour towns gradually became Muslims as Islam developed as the international and interracial religion of the commercial centres in the Near East, Persia and India. In the pre-Islamic Javanese kingdoms of the 15th and 16th centuries, and perhaps even before that time, Muslim traders of mixed descent formed a middle class in society between the Hinduized royalty, nobility and clergy on the one hand and the indigenous country people who tilled the soil on the other.

§ 5.   In the course of time, the Muslim middle class in the harbour towns on the North Coast of Java came to power and the previous rulers who were vassals of the king of Majapahit were killed or expelled. In some places the local nobility was converted to Islam and fraternized with Muslim families.

§ 6.   The religion of the first Muslim communities in the harbour towns on the North Coast was influenced by the ideas of the great mystics of Islam. Pious Javanese of the 17th century and later believed that Islam was spread in Java by the activity of a group of nine saints (the Wali Sanga), who had their centre at the holy mosque of Děmak. Each saint supposedly had his own ideas on Islamic mysticism. This tradition is, however, unreliable. In all likelihood, scholars of divinity and mysticism who wandered through the world of Islam as was usual at the time, availed themselves of the opportunity to settle down as spiritual guides at the new Muslim Courts in Java, where their wordly wisdom was also appreciated. The conversion of the interior of the country proceeded slowly.

§ 7.   The holy mosque of Děmak, the centre of the nine saints, occupies an important place in pious Javanese tradition. Many rather phantastic tales are told about its foundation. The veneration felt by the pious for the holy mosque from the 16th century to the present is due to the fact that it was the religious centre of the first Muslim kingdom in Java, the Sultanate of Děmak.

Chpt. 2.   *Děmak at the end of the 15th and in the first half of the 16th century*

§ 1.   Děmak owes its prominent place in Javanese history partly to its situation. It had a good harbour in the shelter of mount Murya in the 15th century. In the course of time, however, the harbour silted up.

§ 2.   West Javanese (Banten) tradition, dating from the 17th century, is more trustworthy on the history of Děmak than the Central Javanese (Mataram) tradition, which is biased in favour of the dynasty of Mataram. The West Javanese tradition is in accordance with the information on the beginnings of the kingdom of Děmak given by the early-16th century Portuguese traveller Tomé Pires in his Suma Oriental.

§ 3. The ancestor of the line of Muslim rulers of Dĕmak appears to have been a Muslim immigrant of Chinese origin who landed first in Grĕsik (East Java), later settled in Dĕmak and grew rich by trade. During his life, in the last quarter of the 15th century, he acknowledged the suzerainty of the local infidel ruler of Dĕmak and the king of Majapahit. The later but unreliable Central Javanese tradition gives him the name Radèn Patah (Arabic Fattāḥ, Victor). He was said to be born in Palémbang to a Chinese woman from the king of Majapahit's zenana.

§ 4. The successor to this first Muslim settler of Dĕmak (living in the beginning of the 16th century) seems to have brushed aside the local non-Muslim ruler in order to establish a Muslim administration. Nevertheless, he still acknowledged the Shiwaitic-Buddhist king of Majapahit as his sovereign. He is best known as pangéran Sumangsang. He maintained relations with Palémbang.

§ 5. He was succeded by the most important Muslim ruler of Dĕmak, pangéran (later Sultan) Tranggana. His reign (probably 1504-1546) covered a period of important changes in the Archipelago.

§ 6. In 1511 Malaka was conquered by the Portuguese, and in 1512-'13 the attempt of a Javanese admiral to oust them failed, and his fleet was destroyed. Portuguese annalists call the infortunate admiral Paté Unus, ruler of Japara. He is not mentioned in Javanese historical tradition. He may have been a brother-in-law of pangéran Tranggana of Dĕmak. He had probably already died in 1521.

§ 7. The Muslim rulers of Dĕmak were patrons of the growing community of men of religion and pious traders (many of them of mixed Javanese and foreign descent) centring around the mosque. The first imāms of the Dĕmak mosque are said to have been relatives of radèn Rahmat of Ngampèl Dĕnta (Surabaya, see chpt. 1, § 1). His eldest son, in Javanese tradition known as sunan Bonang, may have been the first imām. The fourth and the fifth incumbents used their influence with pangéran Tranggana to make him renounce his allegiance to the infidel king of Majapahit. The fifth imām, called pangulu, founded the "holy city" Kudus and became known to history as the first sunan of Kudus.

§ 8. Pangéran Tranggana took the Islamic title of Sultan probably about 1524, on the insistence of a Sumatran man of religion, who had made the pilgrimage to Mecca and who afterwards became the first sunan of Gunung Jati (Cĕrbon).

§ 9. Javanese traditions about Majapahit history in the 15th century

are unreliable, but the information provided by the Portuguese traveller Tomé Pires seems credible. The most powerful man in the Majapahit kingdom about 1500 was the grand-vizier, whom Pires calls Gusté Paté. The interior of East Java and a part of Central Java were under his control, and he maintained the king's authority over the numerous vassals who ruled in petty states throughout the country.

§ 10.   The Javanese tradition about the fall of the "heathen" capital in 1478 is unreliable. The Majapahit kingdom held out until 1527. A previous attack by a host of Muslim fanatics led by the pangulu of the Děmak mosque was repulsed, and the pangulu (the fourth imām) was killed in battle. The capital finally fell to the pious warriors in a "holy war", led by the fifth pangulu (sunan Kudus) supported by companies of soldiers sent by various Muslim rulers. Tranggana, who had called himself Sultan of Děmak since 1524, was persuaded to act as a Muslim sovereign, the successor of the "heathen" Majapahit king who had disappeared (see § 8).

§ 11.   Some districts of West Java were brought under the control of the new Muslim sovereign of Děmak at an early date, including Cěrbon on the North Coast and Pasir in the interior of the country, in the basin of the Sěrayu river.

§ 12.   Sultan Tranggana extended his authority over many states in East Java, in the interior of the country and on the North Coast, both Shiwaitic-Buddhist states and those already Islamized, which had been ruled by vassals of the Majapahit king before.

§ 13.   The young Islamic kingdom of Děmak exercised authority in several overseas states in Sumatra (Palémbang) and Borneo (Bañjar Masin).

§ 14.   The inland districts of Central Java south and south-east of mount Měrapi, Pěngging and Pajang, were of small economic importance to the trading kingdom of Děmak on the North Coast. Those districts were Islamized through the activities of men of religion whom afterwards Javanese tradition called sèh Lěmah Abang (or Siti Jěnar) and sunan Těmbayat. Sèh Lěmah Abang was a heterodox mystic. He was burned on the pyre, and his disciple the ruler of Pěngging was killed by the strict and severe sunan Kudus, the conqueror of Majapahit.

§ 15.   During a military expedition to the far-off East Javanese state of Panarukan in 1546 sultan Tranggana of Děmak died or was killed.

§ 16.   The organization of the young Islamic kingdom of Děmak in the first half of the 16th century was a replica of the administration of the "heathen" Court of Majapahit. Having moved in Court-circles as vassals

of the king for many years before their rebellion, the rulers of the North
Coast Muslim states were well-acquainted with Majapahit civilization
and Old Javanese literature. Several elements of the pre-Islamic Court
administration were passed on from 15th-century Majapahit to the
16-th and 17th-century Islamic Courts of Pajang and Mataram through
the intermediary of Děmak (and Surabaya). Islamic religious ceremonies
and law were integrated gradually into Děmak Court culture.

Chpt. 3. *Decline and fall of the sultanate of Děmak in the second half of the 16th century*

§ 1. The history of Sultan Tranggana's successors on the throne of
Děmak is imperfectly known. Some West Javanese (Bantěn) traditions
provide partially reliable information.

§ 2. The next ruler of Děmak is called sunan Prawata in Javanese
tradition. He was a man of religion. In 1549 he was murdered by one
of his relatives, Arya Panangsang of Jipang, who aspired to be king.

§ 3. The murderer was punished by another relative known in Javanese
tradition as Jaka Tingkir, afterwards sultan of Pajang, who eventually
became the most powerful man in Central Java. The temporal power
of sunan Prawata's successor in Děmak (called pangéran Kaḍiri)
dwindled, although his spiritual authority still was acknowledged by
the pious. The last semi-independent ruler of Děmak, pangéran Kaḍiri's
successor, was called pangéran Mas or pangéran Juru. He left his
country and fled to his kinsman the ruler of Bantěn in 1588 or 1589,
because paněmbahan Sénapati of Mataram, a homo novus, had usurped
the throne of Pajang.

§ 4. During the reigns of the kings of Mataram who were Sénapati's
successors in the 17th century, Děmak was administered as a province
of the Mataram kingdom by appointed governors. The harbour of
Děmak silted up, but the mosque and the graves of holy men continued
to attract pilgrims from many districts of Java.

Chpt. 4. *History of the smaller states on the North Coast of Central Java in the 16th century: Paṭi and Juwana.*

§ 1. These towns are situated on the east side of the estuary which,
until it silted up, had separated mount Murya from the Javanese main-
land. Děmak and Japara are on the west side. Paṭi and Juwana are
mentioned in Central Javanese mythic tales.

§ 2. Cajongam, which is mentioned in Tomé Pires' Suma Oriental, is to be identified with Juwana. Javanese historical tradition contains some references to Pati. Dĕmak and Pati were rivals in the sea-borne trade along the North Coast of Java. In this contest Dĕmak and Japara ultimately won, while Pati and Juwana lost.

§ 3. After the disintegration of the kingdom of Dĕmak in the middle of the 16th century, Pati was given by the new king of Pajang to one of his captains called ki Pañjawi. Successors of ki Pañjawi, known as Pragola I and II, ruled in Pati in the second half of the 16th century. The relations between the ruling families of Mataram and Pati were at first good but became strained when the ambition of the Mataram rulers became apparent. At last Pati was overrun and ruined by an expeditionary force sent by sultan Agung of Mataram in 1627. The Pragola family disappeared.

Chpt. 5. *History of the smaller states in the North of Central Java*
in the 16th century: Kudus

§ 1. The capital of the Majapahit kingdom was attacked for the first time by a host of Muslim fanatics led by the pangulu of the Dĕmak mosque. The attack was repulsed and the pangulu, known to posterity as Rahmatu' llahi, was slain in battle as a "shāhid" (martyr) in 1524.

§ 2. His son took revenge. Majapahit was captured and sacked by the Muslims in 1527. The young pangulu returned to Dĕmak a hero but eventually quarrelled with Sultan Tranggana and sunan Kali Jaga (another man of religion, from a Tuban family). In the 1540s he decided to found a "holy city" of his own, Kudus (al-Quds, the Arabic name of Jerusalem). Sunan Kali Jaga was his successor as pangulu of the Dĕmak mosque.

§ 3. Sunan Kudus was an energetic man and a fervent Muslim. He made Kudus into a centre of Islamic studies.

§ 4. Sunan Kudus and his two successors were important men in Central Javanese politics during the reigns of the later kings of Dĕmak and of the king of Pajang. But the ambition of the new kings of Mataram was fatal for Kudus, Dĕmak and Pajang alike. The last independent ruler of Kudus left his country and fled to East Java about 1590. Henceforth Kudus and Dĕmak were administered together by appointed governors sent by the Mataram court.

Chpt. 6. *History of the smaller states on the North Coast of Central Java: Japara / Kali Nyamat*

§ *1.* Japara, situated at the foot of mount Murya (which was originally an island) has a better harbour than Děmak. It was the residence of traders during the reign of the most important ruler of Děmak, Sultan Tranggana. The Javanese fleet which was sent to oust the Portuguese from Malaka, but which was defeated in 1512-'13, set out from Japara.

§ *2.* Kali Nyamat is an inland residence not far from Japara, founded according to Javanese tradition by a shipwrecked Chinese sea-captain who was converted to Islam and married a Děmak princess. He was killed in the troubles following the unexpected death of Sultan Tranggana in 1546.

§ *3.* His widow was an energetic woman, called Ratu Kali Nyamat by posterity, who ruled Japara during the second half of the 16th century. She was the grand old lady of the Děmak family, and her influence extended as far as Bantěn. Japara trade flourished, although some further attempts to conquer Malaka for Islam were successfully resisted by the Portuguese.

§ *4.* Having no children of her own, Ratu Kali Nyamat was succeeded as ruler of Japara by a nephew, a Bantěn prince. The independence of the state of Japara ended when the Mataram king took the town and sacked it in 1599. The trade of Japara moved to Sěmarang in the second half of the 17th century.

Chpt. 7. *History of the states in West Java in the 16th century: Cěrbon (Cheribon)*

§ *1.* Some East Javanese legends refer to ancient sea-borne relations between the West Javanese states Galuh and Pajajaran and the East Javanese kingdom (e.g. the tale of the foundation of Majapahit by a Sundanese prince, and the Kidung Sunda story of a 14th-century Sundanese expedition to Majapahit). These legends are unreliable, although the existence of ancient relations between the Javanese in the East and the Sundanese in the West is likely.

§ *2.* Bantěn and Cěrbon were the first districts of West Java where Islam was introduced. The first Muslims were traders of mixed blood.

§ *3.* According to Javanese tradition, Cěrbon was Islamized by one of the nine saints (see chpt. 1, § 1), revered by posterity under the name of Sunan Gunung Jati (after the hill near Cěrbon where he is buried). Portuguese authors mention the names Falatehan and Tagaril. From his native Pasei, in Acheh, he made the pilgrimage to Mecca. As a learned man of religion calling himself Nurullah, he became the honoured guest and, indeed, the brother-in-law of Sultan Tranggana of Děmak (about 1525). Tranggana's assumption of the title of Sultan, and his warlike exploits against the "heathen" kingdom of Majapahit and its dependencies in East Java, were perhaps due to the influence of this energetic Mecca-pilgrim. Having founded first a Muslim community in Bantěn, Nurullah later ruled also in Cěrbon. After the death of Sultan Tranggana in 1546, Nurullah decided in the 1550s to move to Cěrbon where he lived a religious life until his death in 1570. His spiritual influence in West Java was great, although probably less than the influence exercised in East Java by his contemporaries the Sunans of Giri/Grěsik.

§ 4.   Cěrbon never developed into an important state. Sunan Gunung Jati's successors, revered as saintly men, maintained fairly good relations both with the Javanese kings of Pajang and Mataram in Central Java and with the new power in West Java, the V.O.C. (Dutch East India Company) of Batavia. In 1705 the Mataram king finally ceded his claim to suzerainty over Cěrbon to the V.O.C. The courts of Sunan Gunung Jati's successors in the town were respected and maintained by means of allowances from the Netherlands East Indian Government up to 1942.

Chpt. 8.   *History of the states in West Java in the 16th century:*
             Bantěn

§ 1.   In the beginning of the 16th century, before the rise of Islamic states, the Shiwaitic-Buddhist kings of Majapahit in East Java and Pajajaran in West Java were considered to be the paramount powers in Java. The capital of Pajajaran was Pakuwan (now Bogor).

§ 2.   The later Sunan Gunung Jati, Sultan Tranggana's brother-in-law, founded a Muslim community in Bantěn about 1525. In 1527 he conquered the harbour of Pakuwan, called Sunda Kalapa, and renamed it Jayakarta (now Jakarta).

§ 3.   After the holy man's move to Cěrbon, Bantěn was ruled by his son Hasanuddin, who is regarded as the first king in Bantěn Javanese tradition. During his reign Bantěn trade flourished. His second son was adopted by Ratu Kali Nyamat of Japara, and eventually became her successor.

§ 4.   Hasanuddin was succeeded in Bantěn by his eldest son Yusup, the king who conquered the "heathen" capital Pakuwan in 1579. He died soon after this success in 1580.

§ 5.   While still a minor, Yusup's son Muhammad was educated by the kadhi of Bantĕn and became a strict religious man. An attempt by Muhammad's uncle, the heir-apparent of Japara, to become king of Bantĕn was successfully resisted by the local aristocracy, which was partly of Sundanese origin, and the tie linking Bantĕn with Central Java was severed. Muhammad was killed during an expedition to Palémbang, which he began on the advice of his kinsman the last king of Dĕmak, who had fled to Bantĕn in 1596 (see chpt. 3, § 3).

§ 6.   During the reign of Muhammad's son and successor, Abdul Kadir, European (especially Dutch and British) traders became frequent visitors at the port of Bantĕn. In 1619 the local ruler of Jakarta, a vassal of the Bantĕn king, surrendered his town to the Dutch V.O.C.; it was now renamed Batavia.

Chpt. 9.   *History of the states in the North Coast districts of East Java: Jipang/Panolan*

§ 1.   The districts situated between the North Coast Range and the Central Range of limestone hills in East Java were the territories of several kingdoms mentioned in Javanese legends. Mĕṇḍang Kamulan, the mythic original Javanese kingdom, is located in this region.

§ 2.   In the middle of the 16th century Jipang/Panolan was the territory of a member of the royal House of Dĕmak called Arya Panangsang. Having been disappointed in his ambitions, he murdered sunan Prawata of Dĕmak, sultan Tranggana's successor. He was killed in the subsequent struggle for the succession in Central Java by the ruler of Pajang, who is known in Javanese tradition as Jaka Tingkir.

§ 3.   Jipang never again became an independent state after the death of Arya Panangsang. The town was fortified by order of the king of Mataram, sultan Pajang's successor, and served as a fortress on the border between the territories of the Mataram and Surabaya rulers, who were rivals in the struggle for hegemony in Java at the end of the 16th century.

§ 4.   Palémbang, in South Sumatra, was ruled by a Javanese family during the 17th and 18th centuries. This family seems to have had some connections with Jipang.

Chpt. 10.   *History of the states in the North Coast districts of East Java: Tuban*

§ 1.   Tuban, nowadays a harbour of no importance, was a well-known centre of trade in antiquity and is mentioned by Chinese authors as early as the 11th century. It was connected with the districts in the lower Bĕngawan basin by a fairly good road leading through the North Coast Range of limestone hills. It is frequently mentioned in Javanese legendary tales.

§ 2.   Although professing Islam since the middle of the 15th century, the rulers of Tuban were still faithful vassals of the "heathen" Majapahit Court in 1513-'14, when the Portuguese traveller Tomé Pires visited the town. The existence of friendly relations between Tuban and Majapahit is also apparent in Javanese historical tradition.

§ 3.   Members of the ruling family of Tuban (of mixed Javanese and Arab blood, according to Javanese tradition) were active in the propagation of Islam in the interior of Central and East Java in the middle of the 16th century. Sunan Kali Jaga, traditionally said to have been the principal of the nine saints (Wali Sanga, see chpt. 1, § 1), was a native of Tuban.

§ 4.   The Muslim ruler of Tuban seems to have remained neutral during the war waged by sunan Kudus and his host of fanatics against "heathen" Majapahit in the 1520s. When Majapahit fell, Tuban acknowledged the suzerainty of Dĕmak. As a faithful ally of the sultan of Pajang, who was the king of Dĕmak's successor, the ruler of Tuban opposed the territorial expansion of the Mataram dynasty, but in vain. In 1619 the town was taken by the Mataram troops and sacked. Henceforth Tuban was ruled by Mataram governors.

Chpt. 11.   *History of the states in the North Coast districts of East Java: Grĕsik/Giri*

§ 1.   Grĕsik, on the straits of Madura at the mouth of the river Bĕngawan, was an important centre of overseas trade from the 14th century. It became prosperous through the activity of Chinese settlers. It is frequently mentioned in Javanese legendary tales.

§ 2.   Tomé Pires in 1513-'14 described Grĕsik as a prosperous town, ruled by two men of foreign extraction, both of whom were Muslims, but who lived in discord.

§ 3.   Javanese historical tradition is explicit on the origin of the Islamic spiritual lords (sunans) who resided in Giri, a hill resort not far from Grěsik, during the 16th and much of the 17th centuries. It seems impossible to connect this family with the two rulers of Grěsik known to Tomé Pires.

§ 4. The first two sunans of Giri, called sunan Satmata and sunan Dalěm, defended their small Islamic state against attacks from the "heathen" Majapahit Court with much energy, according to Javanese historical tradition. After the fall of Majapahit in 1527, sunan Dalěm of Giri seems to have availed himself of the opportunity to bring Grěsik under his rule (about 1535). Henceforth the sunans of Giri commanded the wealth of the prosperous trading town.

§ 5. The long reign in the second half of the 16th century of the fourth sunan of Giri/Grěsik, called sunan Prapèn in Javanese tradition, witnessed the flourishing period of the Islamic "Ecclesiastical State". Dutch contemporaries called the sunans of Giri the "Moorish Popes". Sunan Prapèn exercised considerable influence in Javanese politics. He reached the pinnacle of his fame in 1581, when a great number of Javanese princes were convened in Giri at his suggestion to acknowledge the king of Pajang as Sultan. Sunan Prapèn died at a very advanced age in 1605.

§ 6. The Court of Giri was a centre of the propagation of Islam extending to Lombok, Celebes, Borneo, the Moluccos and Ternate. Local traditions of those islands testify to the high veneration of these Muslims oversea for the "Raja Bukit" (Sunan Giri).

§ 7. Comparing the three Islamic spiritual principalities of Cěrbon, Kudus and Giri which flourished side by side in the 16th century, Cěrbon appears as a centre of religious studies and mysticism in West Java. Its influence survived the political power of sunan Gunung Jati's successors, which was never very great. Kudus owed its fame to the heroic period of the first sunan, the conqueror of Majapahit. It was soon eclipsed by the royal Courts of Děmak, Pajang and Mataram. Nevertheless the citizens of Kudus retained their Islamic self-esteem through the following centuries. Giri was the most wordly and politically the most influential of the three. Men of Chinese extraction and inter-insular traders occupied important places in the town of Grěsik.

Chpt. 12. *History of the states in the North Coast districts of East Java: Surabaya*

§ 1. The delta of the great East Javanese river Brantas was the site of powerful dynasties in antiquity. The kingdom of Janggala or Kahuripan

(Koripan) is famous as the realm of the "Pañji" prince whose marriage with a princess of Kaḍiri upstream is the central theme of an important cycle of tales and plays in Javanese literature.

§ 2. Tomé Pires mentions a Muslim king of Surabaya ruling in 1513-'14, known to the Portuguese as paté Bubat. It seems possible to identify this ruler with the Muslim lord of Tĕrung (a trading town on the Brantas), a vassal of the "heathen" king of Majapahit, who occupies an important place in Javanese historical tradition.

§ 3. The sunan of Ngampèl Dĕnta (see chpt. 1, § 1), the senior of the nine saints of Islam, lived in Surabaya in the second half of the 15th century according to Javanese tradition. He did not rule the state, but was the head of a numerous family of men of religion, who spread Islam in East Java in the first half of the 16th century.

§ 4. The temporal ruler of Surabaya in the first half of the 16th century, although a Muslim, seems to have opposed for a considerable time the ambition of the new Dĕmak king to extend his realm to East Java. Surabaya submitted to Dĕmak only in the 1530s. There is no evidence that the ruling family of Surabaya was descended from the sunan of Ngampèl Dĕnta, though it is likely that the families were related.

§ 5. The East Javanese princes, who acknowledged the king of Surabaya as their leader, were successful in resisting the attempts of the Mataram ruler to subdue them down to the end of the 16th century. The name of the Surabaya king of the time, Jaya Lĕngkara, is known from East Javanese literature.

§ 6. In the second half of the 16th century the Court of Jaya Lĕngkara of Surabaya was a centre of culture where Islamized Old Javanese literature flourished. Compared with Surabaya, the inland Central Javanese Court of the upstart Mataram dynasty was uncultured.

§ 7. Surabaya surrendered to the Mataram forces, supported by a Dutch squadron cruising in the straits of Madura, in 1625. Pangéran Pĕkik, the last Surabaya prince, was forced to live at the Mataram Court and was married to Sultan Agung's sister. He had considerable influence in civilizing the inland Central Javanese kingdom.

Chpt. 13. *History of Madura in the 16th century: West Madura*

§ 1. In Javanese usage "Madura" means West Madura, now the districts of Bangkalan (formerly Aros Baya) and Sampang. East Madura was the territory of the rulers of Sumĕnĕp. The Madurese do not possess an autochthonous historical tradition referring to ancient kings, unlike the Javanese, the Sundanese and the Balinese. According to Madurese tales the island had Javanese rulers, the first of them a Majapahit prince, from the beginning of history.

§ 2.   The Court of Aros Baya, according to Tomé Pires still "heathen" in the second decade of the 16th century, seems to have embraced Islam as a consequence of the fall of the old capital Majapahit in 1527.

§ 3.   The best known ruler of West Madura in the second half of the 16th century was called Pratanu of Lĕmah Ḍuwur. He was a son-in-law of the sultan of Pajang, and he tried to consolidate his dominions, in which numerous kinsmen disputed his authority.

§ 4.   The West Madurese state lost its independence in 1624, after a fierce fight in Sampang between the Madurese gentry and the Javanese invaders sent by Sultan Agung of Mataram. Descendants of the West Madurese dynasty occupied important places at the Mataram Court in the 17th and 18th centuries.

Chpt. 14.   *History of Madura in the 16th century: East Madura*

§ 1.   A ruler of Sumĕnĕp (East Madura) called Wira Raja supported the East Javanese prince Wijaya who founded the capital Majapahit at the end of the 13th century. Wira Raja thereafter became ruler of Lumajang, in the Eastern Corner of Java, thereby establishing a connection between Madura and the opposite Javanese coast.

§ 2.   According to Javano-Madurese tradition, the Court of Sumĕnĕp, related by marriage with the royal family of Dĕmak, embraced Islam in the first half of the 16th century. East Madura and West Madura remained separate, having no common interests.

§ 3.   Sumĕnĕp was an Islamic outpost in the struggle between the Muslim princes of Java (Dĕmak, Pajang, Surabaya) and the "heathen" rulers of the Eastern Corner of Java (Panarukan, Blambangan) who had the support of the powerful Balinese king of Gèlgèl/Klungkung in the second half of the 16th century. The East Madurese state retained its independence until 1624, when the expeditionary force of Sultan Agung of Mataram invaded the island. The last scions of the House of Sumĕnĕp were killed by order of the Sultan.

Chpt. 15.   *History of the Eastern Corner of Java in the 16th century.*
The western part of the Eastern Corner: Pasuruhan

§ 1.   The regions of Singasari, Bangil and Pasuruhan saw many dynastic wars in pre-Islamic times. They formed an important part of the domains of the 14th-century kings of Majapahit.

§ 2.   Information provided by the Portuguese traveller Tomé Pires on the state of "Gamda" in the beginning of the 16th century must refer to the region of the present-day Malang, Singasari and Pasuruhan. The ruler was still "heathen", and acknowledged the suzerainty of the Majapahit king.

§ 3.   Surabaya and Pasuruhan submitted to Sultan Tranggana of Děmak in the 1530s. In Sěngguruh, in the present-day district of Malang, "heathen" opposition to Islamic rule was not suppressed until 1545.

§ 4.   The rulers of Pasuruhan and Surabaya, having first acknowledged the suzerainty of the Sultan of Pajang in 1581, out of fear of the non-Islamic Balinese king to the East, subsequently opposed the new Mataram ruler's ambition to subdue East Java. A late-16th-century ruler of Pasuruhan extended his political influence in the interior of East Java as far as Kaḍiri and Madyun, in opposition to the rising power of paněmbahan Sénapati of Mataram. Pasuruhan became the paramount power in the Eastern Corner of Java when the last "heathen" state, Blambangan, was subdued about the year 1600 in spite of Balinese support.

§ 5.   Mataram forces sent by Sultan Agung took the town of Pasuruhan in 1616. It was made the base for the subsequent successful attacks on Madura and Surabaya in 1624 and 1625.

Chpt. 16.   *History of the Eastern Corner of Java in the 16th century. The central part of the Eastern Corner: from Prabalingga to Panarukan*

§ 1.   The district of Prabalingga has old connections both with the Těnggěr Highlands to the south-west and with Blambangan to the east. It is mentioned in Javanese legendary history.

§ 2.   The central part of the Eastern Corner of Java was visited by the Majapahit king Ayam Wuruk in 1359. The description of this royal tour in the Old Javanese poem Nāgara Kěrtāgama contains interesting information on this region.

§ 3.   Tomé Pires mentions the "heathen" states of "Canjtam" (perhaps to be identified with Gěnḍing, east of Prabalingga), Pajarakan and Panarukan, which were subdued by a powerful king of Blambangan who opposed the spread of Islam eastward. Another "heathen" state in the interior of the country, called "Chamda" by the Portuguese traveller, seems to have occupied the districts of Saḍèng, Pugĕr and Lumajang, which are mentioned in Javanese historical texts.

§ 4. A campaign of Sultan Tranggana of Dĕmak to subdue the "heathen" states in the Eastern Corner of Java was unsuccessful. The sultan seems to have besieged the town of Panarukan, but failed to take it. He died during or after the siege in 1546.

§ 5. Some Roman Catholic missionaries from the Portuguese colony of Malacca visited Panarukan and Blambangan in the second half of the 16th century. They found that Panarukan was a bone of contention between the Muslim rulers of Pasuruhan and Surabaya and the "heathen" king of Blambangan. At the end of the century the Muslims conquered Blambangan.

§ 6. The conquest of Blambangan by the forces of Sultan Agung of Mataram in 1639 was also the end of Panarukan's independence.

Chpt. 17. *History of the Eastern Corner of Java in the 16th century.*
           The far east of the Eastern Corner: Blambangan

§ 1. Blambangan occupies an important place in both East Javanese and Balinese legendary history.

§ 2. According to Tomé Pires' informants, the "heathen" Blambangan kingdom was the most powerful Javanese state east of Surabaya in the first decades of the 16th century.

§ 3. Balinese historical texts concerned with the reign of king Batu Rènggong of Gèlgèl in the middle of the 16th century refer to a ruler of Blambangan who was a relative of the Balinese king. Santa Guna is given as the name of a Blambangan king by European navigators who called at the port in the last quarter of the 16th century. His successor was vanquished by the Muslim king of Pasuruhan at the end of the century.

§ 4. After the conquest of Pasuruhan by the Mataram forces in 1616, Balinese influence in the centre and the far east of the Eastern Corner of Java revived until the Mataram troops took the town of Blambangan in 1639.

Chpt. 18. *History of the state of Palémbang, South Sumatra,*
           in the 16th century

§ 1. The pre-Islamic history of Palémbang is insufficiently known. Palémbang is believed by many scholars to have been the site of a

South Sumatran trading kingdom called Sri Wijaya which already was mentioned in the 7th century. In Javanese legends concerned with the spread of Islam in East Java by foreigners of mixed Sino-Javanese blood, Palémbang occupies an important place (see chpt. 2, §§ 3-4).

§ 2. Tomé Pires mentions a connection between the local Muslim rulers of Palémbang and Jambi and the king of Děmak in the first decades of the 16th century.

§ 3. In the second half of the 16th century, Palémbang was ruled by a new family who had come from Surabaya. It seems that they were related to the House of Jipang in Central Java (see chpt. 9, § 4). Molana Muhammad, a young king of Bantěn, was killed during a siege of Palémbang in 1596. He had undertaken to make war on Palémbang at the suggestion of his kinsman pangéran Mas of Děmak (see chpt. 3, § 3), who was living in exile in Bantěn and nursed a grudge against the Palémbang ruler, a relative of Arya Panangsang of Jipang who had murdered his grandfather Sunan Prawata (see chpt. 3, § 2).

§ 4. After the repulsed attack from Bantěn, the Palémbang rulers sided both with the rising Mataram kingdom in Central Java and with the Dutch V.O.C. in Batavia/Jakarta.

Chpt. 19. *History of the Central-Javanese states of Pajang and Pěngging in the 16th century*

§ 1. The region between mount Lawu and mount Měrapi, the upper basin of the Běngawan (now called after the present-day capital Solo, better Sålå: Surakarta), was politically and economically of small importance in antiquity.

§ 2. Javanese legends concerning the rulers of Pěngging, which is situated on the south-eastern slope of mount Měrapi, are the only available source of information on the 15th century history of this region. The hero of those legendary tales is called Jaka Boḍo or Jaka Sangara; he seems to have been made ruler of Pěngging by a king of Majapahit. He is called Andaya Ningrat in legendary history.

§ 3. In the first half of the 16th century the ruler of Pěngging was converted to Islam by a heterodox mystic who is called kyahi Lěmah Abang in Javanese religious legends. Sunan Kudus, a strict disciplinarian (see chpt. 5, 3) who wished to extirpate pantheistic heresy, visited Pěngging and killed the ruler, who was unwilling to disavow his mystic master's views. Thus the state of Pěngging lost its independence (see chpt. 2, § 14).

§ 4. According to Javanese historical tradition, the Sultan of Pajang, the successor to the kings of Děmak as suzerain in Central Java, belonged to the House of Pěngging. Called in his youth Jaka Tingkir, he served Sultan Tranggana of Děmak as a captain of the guards, married a princess, and revenged the second king's death by making war on his murderer, Arya Panangsang of Jipang (see chpt. 3, § 3).

§ 5. The ruler of Pajang became the principal heir of Sultan Tranggana, the great king of Děmak of the first half of the 16th century. His long reign in the second half of the century was important for the shifting of the centre of royal authority from the coastal provinces (called the Pasisir in Javanese, extending from Děmak to Surabaya) to the interior of the country. He controlled the local rulers of numerous petty inland states from Banyumas to Madyun and, in an assembly of Javanese princes convened at the court of the venerable sunan Prapèn of Giri in 1581, he was acknowledged as Sultan Adi Wijaya.

§ 6. The Court of Pajang was the first centre of Islamic cultural activity in the interior of the country. Javanese literature and art, which had been cultivated at the older Courts in the Pasisir districts, now became known "south of the mountains".

§ 7. The sultan of Pajang's heir apparent when he died in 1587 was called pangéran Běnawa. After some intriguing by outsiders who hoped to be able to supplant him because he was still young, pangéran Běnawa became king of Pajang through the support of paněmbahan Sénapati of Mataram.

§ 8. The political power of the young Mataram dynasty grew so rapidly in the last decade of the 16th century that the state of Pajang soon lost its independence. The rulers became vassals of the kings of Mataram. Nevertheless, there remained opposition in Pajang to Mataram rule. The last scion of the House of Pajang fled to Surabaya after an insurrection which was suppressed by Sultan Agung in 1618.

Chpt. 20. *History of the state of Mataram in the 16th century*

§ 1. The basins of the rivers Opak and Praga, which discharge into the Indian Ocean, were the sites of civilized Indo-Javanese kingdoms flourishing before A.D. 1000. Prambanan was the capital of powerful kings of a remote antiquity, glorified in Javanese legends which cannot, however, stand the test of scholarly criticism.

§ 2. The district of Mataram was apparently deserted by its rulers for unknown reasons and depopulated in the centuries following the year 1000. It was colonized anew by ki Pamanahan, a captain in the service of the king of Pajang, in the middle of the 16th century. Javanese local legends contain some references to the state of the district before that time. They mention Giring, a place in the Southern Hills (Gunung Kidul), as well as holy men living near the mouth of the river Opak, and the goddess of the Southern Ocean who was worshipped on the beach.

§ 3.   Ki Pamanahan is said to have been a descendant of a legendary lord of Séséla, a small district east of Děmak. As ancestor of the House of Mataram, his life became the subject of many legends which cannot be verified. He remained a loyal vassal of the king of Pajang as long as he lived.

§ 4.   After his death in 1584, his son and successor, who is known only as Sénapati, schemed to undermine the Pajang king's authority. The result was that he came to be acknowledged as paramount ruler of both Mataram and Pajang by 1588, only a few years after the death of the old king.

§ 5.   Paněmbahan Sénapati of Mataram extended his rule over most states in Central Java which had belonged to the kingdom of Děmak half a century before.

§ 6.   His conquest of Madyun precipitated a serious conflict with the powerful king of Pasuruhan, whose authority was acknowledged as far west as Kaḍiri.

§ 7.   Sénapati's design to establish his authority in Kaḍiri by supporting a malcontent pretender to the throne in that state failed. The pretender came to live in Mataram, and there spread some knowledge of East Javanese culture at the new inland Court.

§ 8.   The powerful and cultured rulers of the East Javanese states, especially Surabaya and Pasuruhan, did not consider the upstart paněmbahan of Mataram to be their peer. He was not well-connected by marriage. His personal energy and the enthusiastic support of his followers, many of whom were immigrants and adventurers eager for booty, brought considerable success to the aggressive policy of Mataram in the last decades of the 16th century. Sénapati died in 1601.

§ 9.   The Court of Mataram at first had little culture. A civilizing influence was exercised by Sunan Kali Jaga, one of the nine saints (see chpt. 1, § 1) and a member of the ruling family of Tuban who had come to live at the Děmak Court in the first half of the 16th century, and his descendants the spiritual lords of Ngadi Langu (near Děmak).

Chpt. 21. *The cause of the decline of the coastal states of Java in the 16th century*

§ 1. The remarkable success of the young Mataram state in its struggle with the older and more cultured coastal kingdoms for supremacy in Central and East Java was made possible by discord and jealousy among the rival rulers of the towns, which prevented coordinated action to fight off attacks coming from the interior.

§ 2. Moreover, the coastal states were harassed on the seas by the rising power of Portuguese and Dutch traders.

§ 3. The ruling classes of the seaport towns consisted of families of mixed blood, mostly Sino-Javanese and Indo-Javanese. The shared Islamic religion made possible an amalgamation of people of different descent through marriage. There was a cultural and social gap between the well-to-do citizens and nobility of the towns and the inland Javanese, still living in a purely agrarian society. There was no love lost between them. The attacks of the Mataram bands were savage, and the population of several port towns was wilfully decimated. There is also some reason to believe that the state of public health in the densely populated towns on the seacoast was deteriorating because of tropical diseases such as malaria which were spread by the increasing international and interinsular traffic. The resistance of the town-dwellers may have been sapped by illness.

II.

THE REIGN OF SENAPATI INGALAGA OF MATARAM
1575-1601

Summary of:

H. J. de Graaf, De regering van Panembahan Sénapati
Ingalaga. 's-Gravenhage 1954. *Verhandelingen van het
Koninklijk Instituut voor Taal-, Land- en Volkenkunde.*
Vol. 13.

II. PANEMBAHAN SENAPATI OF MATARAM

Chpt. 1 (p. 3). *Javanese sources of historiography*

Chpt. 2 (p. 5). *Kyahi Geḍé Séla, the ancestor of the House of Mataram, his legendary genealogy*

p. 8. There are Javanese legends about Séséla.

p. 10. A fire kindled at a lamp burning on the holy grave at Séséla was brought to the royal residence of Surakarta once a year, probably since its foundation in the 18th century, to symbolise the link between the Court and the legendary place of origin of the Mataram dynasty.

p. 13. Séséla is not mentioned in 17th-century Dutch notes concerning the origin of the dynasty. Dutch authors of the time reflect West Javanese (Bantĕn) tradition, saying that the first Mataram ruler was a man of low origin and a servant of the preceding king of Pajang.

Chpt. 3. *People from Séséla serving in Pajang*

p. 16. There are Javanese legends about Jaka Tingkir, who became king of Pajang, and his Pĕngging origin.

p. 18. Remnants of the royal residence of Pajang can be seen.

p. 19. Legendary tales tell of ki gĕḍé Séséla's son, called ki gĕḍé Ngĕnis, who became a servant of the king of Pajang. He had a son called ki gĕḍé Pamanahan who became the first ruler of Mataram, and also a distant relative, ki Pañjawi, who became the ancestor of the House of Paṭi.

Chpt. 4. *The struggle between Jipang and Pajang*

p. 24. After the death of Sultan Tranggana of Dĕmak, in 1546, his son-in-law the king of Pajang, formerly called Jaka Tingkir, became the most powerful man in the realm. The late king's son contented himself to be a spiritual lord and was called susuhunan Prawata.

p. 26. Arya Panangsang, the ruler of Jipang, pretended to be the only rightful heir to the throne of Dĕmak.

p. 27. His claim was supported by Sunan Kudus, one of the nine saints of Javanese Islam, who is said to have been jealous of the growing influence at the Court of Dĕmak acquired by another man of religion, Sunan Kali Jaga.

p. 29. In 1549 Arya Panangsang had susuhunan Prawata, Sultan

Trangganna's son, and also the king's son-in-law, pangéran Kali Nyamat of Japara, murdered by his emissaries in order to open his way to the throne. His attempt upon the life of the king of Pajang failed.

p. 31. Sunan Kudus' spiritual influence maintained a balance of power between the rulers of Jipang and Pajang for some time.

Chpt. 5. *The queen of Japara, ratu Kali Nyamat, in the second half of the 16th century*

p. 32. Contemporary Portuguese authors testify to ratu Kali Nyamat's power and wealth. She was the widow of the murdered pangéran.

p. 33. During her reign Japara fleets twice attacked Malaka, in 1550 and in 1574, but both times they failed.

p. 35. Being childless, she appointed a nephew, a prince of Bantĕn, to be her heir. This ruler, known as pangéran Japara, did not succeed when he claimed the throne of Bantĕn which fell vacant in 1580, and so the link between the rulers of the two seaport towns was severed. In the history of the Moluccos Japara is mentioned a few times, but the relation with East Java (Giri/Grĕsik) was more important.

p. 37. Desirous of revenge on her husband's murderer, ratu Kali Nyamat supported the ruler of Pajang, her brother-in-law, in his struggle with Jipang, but she had no troops to send into the interior of the country.

Chpt. 6. *The decisive fighting in the Pajang-Jipang war*

p. 39. The 17th-century Javanese historical tradition, which is biassed in favour of the House of Mataram, ascribes all the glory in the killing of Arya Panangsang to ki Pamanahan's young son (the later Sénapati of Mataram). It is doubtful whether the men from Sésela who served the king of Pajang really were such important factors in the war.

p. 42. The Pajang-Jipang war is mentioned by a 17th-century Dutch author.

p. 43. The war ended in 1558. The mosque of Pamantıngan, where ratu Kali Nyamat built a mausoleum for her murdered husband, is dated 1559.

Chpt. 7. *The king of Pajang's reward to the men from Sésela*

p. 44. The 17th-century Mataram tradition says that ki Pamanahan was given the district of Mataram by the king of Pajang, and ki Pañjawi the district of Paṭi, as rewards for their services in the war. This tradition is unreliable.

p. 47. Old West Javanese (Bantĕn) tales refer to ki Pamanahan as an adventurer who, not being highly thought of at the Court of Pajang, settled in Mataram to make his fortune in a new land. This version seems more credible.

Chpt. 8. *Ki gĕḍé Mataram*

p. 49. On their way from Pajang to Mataram, the new settlers met with the lord of Karang Lo, near the place where they crossed the river Opak.

p. 51. Giring, a district of palmsugar tappers in the Southern Hills, was visited by ki Pamanahan. According to Javanese legends, he was acknowledged there as ki gĕḍé Mataram, the predestined ancestor of a long line of kings.

p. 52. The Javanese tales about the settling of Mataram are confusing.

p. 54. There is reason to believe that the first seignorial residence in Mataram (called kraton in Javanese tradition) was completed in 1578, twenty years after the end of the Pajang-Jipang war, and that ki gĕḍé Mataram died in 1584.

Chpt. 9. *The relations between the Central Javanese king of Pajang and East Javanese rulers*

p. 55. Pajang was an inland state. It did not possess the maritime commercial connections with East Java and the other islands which had made the kingdom of Dĕmak prosperous.

p. 56. After the death of Sultan Tranggana of Dĕmak in 1546, Surabaya regained its independence and became the most powerful state in East Java.

p. 57. In the second half of the 16th century West Madura was ruled by the pangéran of Lĕmah Ḍuwur, who is said to have married a Pajang princess. He was not, however, a vassal of the Pajang king.

p. 58. The history of the ruling family of Surabaya in the second half of the 16th century is imperfectly known. The Surabaya rulers never became vassals of the king of Pajang. In the 17th century, however, descendants of this family, having submitted to Mataram rule, occupied important places at the Mataram Court.

p. 60. Giri, near Grĕsik, on the straits of Madura, was ruled by a family of spiritual lords descended from one of the legendary nine saints of Javanese Islam. Sunan Prapèn of Giri, who reigned in the second half of the 16th century, exercised authority in several islands in the eastern part of the Archipelago. A Javanese tale mentioning an intervention by Giri in Kaḍiri in order to maintain Islamic rule, is unverified.

p. 62. The king of Pajang was proclaimed Sultan Adi Wijaya in an assembly of Central and East Javanese rulers convened by sunan Prapèn of Giri in 1581. The ruler of Surabaya became the king's principal ally and representative in East Java.

p. 64. A Javanese tale of the taking of Wirasaba by Pajang forces in 1578 probably refers to a small state in the basin of the Sĕrayu in the present district of Banyumas, and not to the more important state of Wirasaba in East Java.

p. 65. After the victory of the king of Pajang over Jipang in 1558, fugitive members or adherents of the House of Jipang seem to have gone, *via* Surabaya, to Palémbang in South Sumatra, to restore their fortunes. They became the founders of a Javanese dynasty which ruled there until the first decades of the 19th century. This Javano-Palémbang tradition is mentioned by Dutch authors.

p. 67. The authority of the king of Pajang was not recognized as absolute by the rulers of old states like Dĕmak and Japara. A ruler of Dĕmak received envoys sent by the powerful sultan of Acheh to solicit support for an intended attack on Portuguese Malakka, as late as 1564. This fact is mentioned by a Portuguese author. Apparently the name of the inland kingdom of Pajang was not known overseas.

Chpt. 10. *The first three years of the reign of panĕmbahan Sénapati of Mataram*

p. 70. Ki gĕḍé Mataram died in 1584. Mataram Court traditions say that his successor, known as Sénapati Ingalaga, had been adopted as a son by the king of Pajang in his youth.

p. 71. Seventeenth- and eighteenth-century Mataram authors embellished Sénapati's history with many features which cannot be verified. The ambitious young ruler was unwilling to acknowledge the king of Pajang as his master from the beginning of his reign.

p. 72. He seems to have convinced rulers of petty inland states in Kĕḍu and Bagĕlen, north and west of Mataram, to shift their allegiance from the king of Pajang to himself. Only one of them, the master of Bocor, wanted to remain true to Pajang, but he was overruled.

p. 73. Later Mataram authors made much of Sénapati's divine consecration as ancestor of a long line of kings, given him while sleeping on the Stone of Lipura (the centre of the country) and during a visit in the underwater residence of the goddess of the Southern Ocean.

p. 77. He is said to have been visited in Mataram by the king of Pajang's son and son-in-law, who tried to persuade him not to push matters to extremes, but he persisted.

Chpt. 11. *Sénapati's conquest of the royal residence of Pajang*

p. 80. A relative of Sénapati's who had fallen into disgrace with the king was given protection in Mataram. This was the immediate cause of the war.

p. 82. The king of Pajang personally commanded the advance on Mataram despite his age and illness. The royal troops were held up near Prambanan, according to 17th century Mataram authors, who mention an eruption of mount Měrapi as a cause of the king's retreat to Pajang.

p. 85. While visiting the holy grave at Těmbayat, to pray for support, the Pajang king was given to understand by various bad omens that his time had come.

p. 86. Following the retreating troops to the royal residence at Pajang, Sénapati stayed outside to wait, knowing that the king was about to die.

p. 87. Javanese historical tradition ascribes the king's death to one Juru Taman, whose identity is unknown. Perhaps Sénapati took a hand in hastening the demise, or perhaps Juru Taman was the name of a spirit who was believed to have sided with the young ruler against the old king. The year of Sénapati's triumph, A.J. 1509 (A.D. 1587), is inscribed in stone on a gate of the mosque of Kuṭa Gěḍé, the first capital of the Mataram kings.

Chpt. 12. *Děmak interlude*

p. 91. Sultan Adi Wijaya was buried in Butuh. Authority over Pajang was given to the king of Děmak, a son-in-law of the deceased ruler. The sultan's young son, called pangéran Běnawa, was made ruler of Jipang. This arrangement is ascribed to the spiritual lord of Kudus, a descendant of one of the legendary nine saints of Javanese Islam.

p. 92. Dĕmak rule caused discontent among the Pajang gentry. Pangéran Bĕnawa, feeling slighted and wanting to return to Pajang, sought Sénapati's support.

p. 94. As the Mataram forces advanced upon Pajang, the king was deserted by his troops, who were partly half-Chinese mercenaries, and the Pajang gentry. The king of Dĕmak was forced to return to his own country.

p. 96. Pangéran Bĕnawa's reign in Pajang did not last long. He seems to have abdicated, and Pajang became a province of the Mataram kingdom.

p. 97. The king of Dĕmak left his country forever in 1588 as he could not stand against the invading Mataram forces. After some wandering about he came to live in exile at the court of his kinsman the king of Bantĕn. Dĕmak also became a province of the Mataram kingdom.

p. 99. Sénapati first appointed one of his younger brothers as his governor in Pajang, in 1588. Shortly thereafter a son of the unlucky pangéran Bĕnawa was made ruler of Pajang under Sénapati's suzerainty. He resided in Pajang from 1591 to 1617.

p. 101. Since his triumph over the king of Dĕmak in 1588 Sénapati seems to have borne the title of panĕmbahan of Mataram. He gave his brothers pangéran titles referring to districts in East Java where he had no authority whatever: Pugĕr, Singasari, Juminah (= Blitar), Purbaya (= Madyun). He seems to have intended to add those districts to his kingdom.

Chpt. 13. *Sénapati's efforts to win the hegemony in East Java.*
           His years of success

p. 104. The late king of Pajang's authority had been acknowledged in East Java to a certain extent since 1581, and the new panĕmbahan of Mataram, his successor in Central Java, hoped to follow in his predecessor's footsteps. In 1589 Sénapati ordered his Central Javanese vassals to follow him into East Java. He was held up in the district of Japan (= Majakĕrta) by the East Javanese rulers who were led by the king of Surabaya. Before things came to a head, the spiritual lord of Giri (a descendant of one of the nine saints of Javanese Islam) prevailed upon the rivals to return to their countries without joining battle. Eighteenth-century Javanese historians say that a riddle propounded by the holy man and solved by each of the opposing princes in his own way was an important factor at the meeting in Japan.

p. 107. The rivalry between Mataram and Surabaya erupted in a quarrel over the district of Waru (Blora) and in the Madyun war. The ruler of Madyun was a member of the royal family of Dĕmak, and an opponent of Sénapati's policy of expansion. In Javanese romanticized history the king of Madyun is said to have neglected the defence of his kingdom under the influence of a beautiful concubine who had been sent by Sénapati. In the war, which began with an incursion by Mataram into Madyun territory, the Madyun forces and some Surabaya auxiliaries were defeated (in 1590). The king fled to Surabaya. On his entering into the royal residence of Madyun Sénapati captured a young princess who had remained there. He took her by force, and afterwards she became one of his principal wives. This was the first marriage alliance between the young Mataram family and the old royal House of Dĕmak. Javanese historians therefore made much of it.

p. 112. The ruler of Kanitèn, situated not far from Madyun, was a true vassal of the king of Pasuruhan, and tried to hold up Sénapati's advance. But he was defeated in 1591.

p. 114. The districts north and west of Mataram, in Kĕdu and Bagĕlèn, were ruled by faithful followers of the Mataram family in the last decade of the 16th century. The kingdom of Cĕrbon in West Java was never attacked, and relations were fairly friendly.

Chpt. 14. *The last decade of Sénapati's reign. Years of adversity*

p. 117. In Kaḍiri an aged ruler died and there followed a quarrel over the succession. Sénapati tried to establish his authority in that important East Javanese state by supporting one of the pretenders, but in 1591 the other pretender won with the support of the king of Surabaya. The loser came to live in exile at the Mataram court, and henceforth was called Sénapati Kaḍiri.

p. 119. The Mataram king took advantage of the accomplishments of the cultured Kaḍiri prince by making him supervise the building of a town-wall.

p. 121. The East Javanese rulers combined forces to make war on Mataram from 1593 to 1595. They pressed far into Pajang territory but did not reach Mataram proper. Sénapati Kaḍiri was killed fighting his East Javanese kinsmen.

p. 123. Mataram attacked the North Coast trading town of Tuban without success in 1598 and 1599. The first Dutch navigators visiting Java at that time found Tuban a flourishing community ruled by a powerful king.

p. 125. Kali Nyamat, the residence of the king of Japara, was taken by Mataram invaders in 1599. The defeated ruler was a descendant of the great Sultan Tranggana of Děmak.

p. 127. The king of Pati (and Juwana) on the North Coast was Sénapati's brother-in-law. He marched on Mataram to check his kinsman's ambition, but in vain. He died in the attempt in 1600.

p. 128. Sénapati died in 1601 (the year of a complete eclipse of the sun) in Kajěnar, in the present district of Sragèn, having designated his son Jalang to succeed him as king of Mataram although he was still a minor.

Addenda: a Dutch summary, a list of dates (1546-1601), genealogies of the royal families of Děmak-Pajang and Mataram, a Dutch bibliography and a Dutch register of names.

III.

THE REIGN OF SULTAN AGUNG OF MATARAM
1613-1645

AND HIS PREDECESSOR PANEMBAHAN SEDA-ING-KRAPYAK
1601-1613

Summary of:

H. J. de Graaf, De regering van Sultan Agung, vorst van Mataram, 1613-1645, en die van zijn voorganger Panembahan Séda-ing-Krapjak, 1601-1613. 's-Gravenhage 1958. *Verhandelingen van het Koninklijk Instituut voor Taal-, Land- en Volkenkunde.* Vol. 23.

III. SULTAN AGUNG OF MATARAM

Chpt. 1. *The reign of panĕmbahan Séda-ing-Krapyak, 1601-1613*

p. 1. Sénapati's successor was a younger son by the princess of Paṭi. His elder sons were from women of lesser rank. The second panĕmbahan is known only by his posthumous name Séda-ing-Krapyak.

p. 2. The eldest surviving son, who had been given the honorary name of pangéran of Pugĕr, was made governor of Dĕmak. He rose in rebellion against his younger brother out of spite, and was supported by the king of Surabaya. Some notes by the Dutch admiral Jacob van Heemskerck, who touched at the ports of Dĕmak and Surabaya in 1602, refer to these events. Pangéran Pugĕr was defeated by Mataram troops but was pardoned in 1605.

p. 9. Another brother of the king, called pangéran Jaga Raga, was made governor of Panaraga, south of Madyun. In 1608 he was recalled to Mataram and banished to a distant island before the rebellion he had begun became dangerous.

p. 12. The state of Surabaya was ruled around 1600 by a king who may have been a distant relative of sunan Ngampèl Dĕnta, one of the legendary nine saints of Javanese Islam.

p. 13. A Dutch description of Surabaya in 1620 gives an idea of the strength of the fortifications and the power of the king.

p. 16. Early 17th-century Dutch diaries and letters provide information on the expansion of the Surabaya king's sphere of authority in East Java and the outer islands.

p. 18. The letters from the Dutch East India Company (V.O.C.) trading post at Grĕsik, north of Surabaya, frequently mention inland wars between Mataram and Surabaya. The Grĕsik factory was closed in 1615.

p. 20. Mataram harassed the districts of Surabaya and Grĕsik with annual incursions from 1610 to 1613. The town of Grĕsik was taken and sacked in 1613.

p. 22. During the reign of panĕmbahan Séda-in-Krapyak there was considerable building activity in the capital of the prosperous Mataram kingdom. There is also mention of some literary and theatrical developments led by the ḍalang (wayang performer) Pañjang Mas, a native of Kĕḍu.

p. 24. The king of Mataram sought relations with the Dutch traders, which resulted in the founding of a V.O.C. factory in Japara in 1613. In the same year the king met with an accident and died in his game-preserve (Krapyak). His posthumous name Séda-ing-Krapyak refers to this event.

Chpt. 2. *Sultan Agung's first conquests, 1613-1619*

p. 26. After the king's death there was some hesitation about the succession. A younger son who had a good claim was forced to resign, and the eldest son, called pangéran Rangsang, who was born of a princess of the House of Pajang, was made king. The name Sultan Agung, by which he is known in history, was given him by historians after his death. He took the title of Sultan in 1641.

p. 28. The new king continued the war with the East Javanese rulers by sending his warriors on a raid into the Eastern Corner ("Oost-hoek") of Java in 1614. The district of Pasuruhan was by-passed, and the Mataram troops reached Lumajang.

p. 30. Returning home to Mataram laden with booty, the raiders were pursued by East Javanese forces, mainly from Surabaya and Madura. Retreating behind the river Andaka (Brantas) the Mataram troops gave battle and inflicted such severe losses upon their enemies that the pursuit was abandoned. The rest of the raiders reached Mataram in triumph in the last months of 1614.

p. 32. Sultan Agung personally took command of the army which captured the fortified town of Wirasaba (now called Maja Agung) on the Brantas in 1615. The young ruler of Wirasaba was insufficiently supported by the king of Surabaya, who was quarreling with other East Javanese kings at the time of the siege.

p. 35. Roused from the preoccupation with their quarrels by the loss of the important fortress of Wirasaba, the East Javanese rulers led a campaign right into the centre of the Mataram kingdom. Starting from Lasĕm on the North Coast their forces advanced southward. Sultan Agung prevented the men of Pajang from going over to the enemy, as the invaders had hoped they would, and the East Javanese forces were defeated near Siwalan in the district of Pajang in 1616.

p. 39. Sultan Agung appointed some military men to high adminis-trative posts because of the imminent danger to the centre of his kingdom during these years.

p. 40. The town of Lasĕm on the North Coast, from which the East Javanese campaign had started in 1616, was taken and sacked before the end of same year. Dutch V.O.C. ships supported the Mataram king at the time.

p. 41. The campaign in the Eastern Corner of 1614 was repeated in 1617. The town of Pasuruhan was taken this time and its ruler fled to Surabaya.

p. 43. The insurrection in the district of Pajang, which had been imminent since 1616, broke out in 1618. The insurgent, a descendant of the Sultan of Pajang who had been paramount king in Central Java fifty years before, was defeated and fled to Surabaya. His expectations of support from a discontented faction at the Mataram court and the still independent ruler of Tuban were not fulfilled. The town of Pajang was taken and razed to the ground, and its people were marched to Mataram to work for the king.

p. 48. The important trading-town of Tuban, on the North Coast, was taken and destroyed in 1619. Again the support given to the besieged fortress by Surabaya and Madura was insufficient. This victory made Sultan Agung master of a considerable part of the eastern North Coast districts, extending to the boundaries of Surabaya. Meanwhile the Dutch V.O.C. had been busy establishing trading-posts in various places on the coast.

Chpt. 3.   *Relations between Sultan Agung of Mataram and the V.O.C. from 1613-1624*

p. 53. Sultan Agung made friendly advances towards the V.O.C., who had a trading-post in Grĕsik, soon after his accession to the throne in 1614. He considered the V.O.C. to be a useful ally in his struggle with the rulers of the coastal states, especially the king of Surabaya.

p. 54. A trading-post was established in Japara, on the territory of the Mataram king and partly at his expense, in 1615. Sultan Agung received 4 pieces of ordnance, two of them valuable brass cannon, in return. The trading-post at Grĕsik was closed.

p. 56. The unsatisfactory condition of the Japara trading-post led to the sending of envoys to the Mataram court in 1616 and 1618. They had little success.

p. 58. The trading-post was taken by surprise and the Dutch traders were arrested by order of the king in 1618. Some were killed. The V.O.C. servants were charged with illicit practices in trade and bad behaviour. Sultan Agung considered them to be his subjects as long as they resided in his territory. He began to be aware of the danger of

the Dutch presence by the developments at Jakarta and through the
warnings of British traders.

p. 60. The events at Japara led to a terrible revenge by the Dutch
admiral Jan Pieterszoon Coen. He twice attacked and burned the town
in 1618 and 1619. The British trading-post in Japara was destroyed
and the Chinese traders were forced to move to Jakarta, where they
were regarded as V.O.C. subjects. After this calamity Japara was
provided with fortifications by order of the king.

p. 64. J. P. Coen re-established a small trading-post at Grěsik in
1619, promising the king of Surabaya support in his struggle with
Sultan Agung of Mataram.

p. 65. Several Dutch traders who had been arrested in Japara in
1618 were kept prisoner by the Javanese authorities. They were con-
fined to a military post in the interior of the country, where they led
a miserable life.

p. 67. The liberation of the Dutch prisoners was one of the issues
of the negotations between Sultan Agung and the Governor General
which went on for years. Another issue was the supply of Javanese rice,
which the V.O.C. posts and ships needed in great quantities. The parties
came to an understanding in 1622, mainly because the king wanted
V.O.C. support, or at least neutrality, in his war with Surabaya. The
prisoners were released.

p. 72. V.O.C. envoys sent to the Mataram court in 1622, 1623 and
1624 with various presents (including Persian horses) were graciously
received. Slowly each side began to understand the other's interests
more clearly.

Chpt. 4. *Sultan Agung's war on Surabaya, 1620-'25, and his victory*

p. 77. The strategic situation of the town of Surabaya, between
branches of the river Brantas, and its strong fortifications made it impossible for the Mataram troops to storm it with their usual aggressive
tactics.

p. 78. Sultan Agung's first and second campaigns against Surabaya
in 1620 and 1621 were unsuccessful, partly because V.O.C. ships cruising
on the coast prevented the king's proas from sailing farther eastward
than Tuban. They did not reach the straits of Madura, where they
could have victualled the king's land forces. Therefore Sultan Agung
decided to come to an understanding with the V.O.C.

p. 79. In 1622 Sukadana, a trading-town on the South Coast of
Borneo and an outpost of the Surabaya king's trading empire, was

taken by Sultan Agung's governor in Kĕndal, a port on Java's North Coast west of Sĕmarang.

p. 81. Mataram troops took and destroyed the towns of Grĕsik and Jortan on the straits of Madura in 1622. There were no V.O.C. ships to interfere. The country surrounding Surabaya was devastated far and wide.

p. 82. The 1623 campaign against Surabaya was again unsuccessful.

p. 83. The rulers of the states of Madura (Sampang, Bangkalan, and Sumĕnĕp), who were on the side of the king of Surabaya, were defeated by Mataram invaders in 1624. There was fierce fighting in several places. The ruling families were extirpated or fled to Bantĕn and Giri. Only the ruler of Bangkalan was spared. He was henceforth forced to live at the Court of Mataram.

p. 93. The town of Surabaya was besieged from the land-side beginning in 1624. Supplies from allies overseas were scarce because of the hostile presence of V.O.C. ships in the straits of Madura. The Mataram forces blocked the water supply and spoiled the water of the river, but did not try to storm the fortifications. The blind and aged king of Surabaya had the sense to surrender without fighting in 1625. He was allowed to reside in his town until his death. His son, called pangéran Pĕkik in history, was henceforth forced to live in Mataram. He married Sultan Agung's sister and, being a man of culture, did much to civilize the Court of the inland kingdom.

Chpt. 5. *Sultan Agung's character and behaviour, the royal residence of Mataram, and the administration of the kingdom*

p. 99. Reports from Dutch envoys who visited Mataram in the first half of the 17th century provide reliable and substantial information on Sultan Agung and his Court. The Dutch reports are supported by Javanese historical records. Sultan Agung's religion became gradually more orthodox as he advanced in life. He tried to force Dutch prisoners to be circumcised and to become Muslims.

p. 104. The royal residence, called Karta, was enlarged and rebuilt several times during Sultan Agung's reign.

p. 113. The king took care of the central mosque of the realm, where he worshipped regularly.

p. 116. The central administration of the kingdom was entrusted to a limited number of high officials, who were removed from office and even killed if they did not give satisfaction. The principal official

was the grandvizier (patih). The princes of the royal blood had no
regular functions in the administration, and were obliged to live in the
capital. The outlying provinces, formerly independent states, were
under governors who travelled at least once a year to Mataram to pay
tribute and receive orders. Some governors of coastal provinces were
of foreign origin.

p. 120. The village subjects of the Mataram king were liable to
taxes in kind, statute labour and military service, but some were exempt
from some or all duties. The incomes of the royal household, the princes
of the blood and the officers of state came from villages and districts
which were allotted to them as appanages.

p. 121. The king maintained contact with the courtiers by means
of frequent gatherings where no one was allowed to be absent. Non-
attendance was severely punished. Hunting was the royal pastime.

p. 125. Within the army the royal bodyguard and the garrisons of
some posts and fortresses were regular soldiers, divided into a number
of companies. The villagers who were liable to military service could
be called up if necessary, but their fighting-value was not great.

Chpt. 6. *The title of Susuhunan of Mataram, borne since 1624*

p. 127. V.O.C. records are explicit that the new title was adopted
after the conquest of Madura. It was originally a spiritual title, belonging
to the legendary nine saints of Javanese Islam.

p. 129. The cannon called Pañcawura, the biggest piece of ordnance ever founded in Indonesia, is dated 1625. It was also a mark
of the Mataram king's rising power. It is now in Surakarta.

p. 131. The whole of Java was afflicted by terrible epidemics during
the years 1625-1627. A considerable part of the population was swept
away, but the nature of the illness is unknown.

p. 132. The king of Mataram had planned to make war on Bantĕn,
west of Jakarta/Batavia, as early as 1625-'26. He could not proceed
because the V.O.C. government refused him the support he needed.
This made him bitter towards the V.O.C.

Chpt. 7. *The Pati war, 1627*

p. 135. The ruling family of Pati, on the North Coast, was related
by marriage to the House of Mataram.

p. 136. A renewal of the traditional relations between the two families by the marriage of a very young pair was necessary to avert the outbreak of hostilities in 1624.

p. 137.   Nevertheless, the ruler of Paṭi, the last king in Central Java who was independent of the susuhunan of Mataram, did not resign himself to vassalage. Relying on support from a discontented faction at the Mataram Court, he organized an insurrection in the North Coast districts. The susuhunan himself took command of the troops who marched on Paṭi and quelled the revolt in 1627. The district of Paṭi was laid waste, and the ruling family was extirpated.

Chpt. 8.   *The siege of Batavia in the years 1628 and 1629*

p. 144.   After 1625, the fall of Surabaya, relations between the Mataram Court and the V.O.C. government in Jakarta/Batavia became strained, mainly because the king now regarded himself as paramount ruler of the whole of Central and East Java and Madura. Considering the foreigners to be his subjects so long as they resided in his territories, he resented fiercely any neglect of ceremony and particularly any interruption of the annual visits of envoys offering presents, which he felt were his due. The V.O.C. government did not see annual embassies as an obligation, and resented the casual Javanese handling of matters of commerce which were of the highest importance to the Dutch.

p. 145.   After the fall of Surabaya and Paṭi in 1625 and 1627, the king felt it was time to attack the intractable foreign settlers in Batavia. Having closed the North Coast ports to all traffic, he sent a sea-borne force from Tĕgal and two army corps, from Kĕndal and Mataram, overland to attack the town in 1628. The attacks were repulsed by the Dutch and their foreign auxiliaries (Ambonese, Chinese and even Japanese). Several Javanese commanders were killed in battle and others were executed as punishment for their failure to take the town. The rest of the army returned to Mataram at the end of 1628.

p. 149.   A second attack on Batavia was planned for 1629. The Javanese forces brought heavy artillery and placed it in position to bombard the town. There was fierce fighting at several points. In the end the Javanese commanders were obliged to abandon the attempt, mainly because of the scarcity of victuals. The military stores in Tĕgal had been discovered and burned by a squadron of V.O.C. ships even before the Javanese troops appeared before Batavia. The terrible losses among the retreating Javanese were mainly caused by exhaustion and famine. The small V.O.C. forces were not in a position to follow up their success by a pursuit into the unexplored interior of West Java. The valuable artillery was brought safely back to Mataram. The energetic Dutch commander Jan Pieterszoon Coen, the founder of Batavia, died of an intestinal trouble during the last days of this second siege.

p. 152. The events of the unsuccessful attacks on Batavia were described by several Javanese and Dutch contemporaries. The identity of many Javanese officers and princes who took part in the war can be ascertained by comparing tales and reports from both sides.

Chpt. 9. *The relations between the Mataram Court and the Portuguese government in Malaka and Goa, 1629-'34*

p. 164. The Portuguese in Malaka maintained their position in the northern part of the Archipelago and on the Sumatra coast with energy and not without success. An attack by the Achehnese sultan Iskandar Muda on Malaka was repulsed with heavy losses for the Sumatran fleet in 1629, and some V.O.C. ships were taken and burned in the Jambi river on the coast of Sumatra by a Portuguese squadron in 1630, even though the Dutch captains were assisted by the Jambi ruler's coastal batteries.

p. 165. Portuguese envoys were received graciously at the Mataram Court in 1631. They promised the support of a squadron of Portuguese ships cruising along the Java coast when Sultan Agung's next attack on Batavia was due.

p. 168. Envoys sent by Sultan Agung (in a Portuguese ship) to the viceroy in Goa in 1632 are mentioned in Portuguese reports. It was agreed that the town of Batavia, if taken by the joint efforts of Javanese and Portuguese forces, would be turned over to the viceroy.

p. 170. Exchange of envoys between Mataram and Malaka/Goa was repeated in 1632-'34. The Portuguese power was declining, however, and it was impossible for them to keep their promises.

Chpt. 10. *The relations between the Mataram Court and the V.O.C. government in Batavia, 1629-'34*

p. 173. After the unsuccessful attacks on Batavia of 1628 and 1629, the king showed some inclination to restore peaceful relations with the V.O.C. if qualified envoys with valuable presents were sent to Mataram.

The V.O.C. government distrusted the king's intentions and was unwilling to sue for peace. So nothing came from it.

p. 177. The rumour of an agreement between the Mataram Court and the Portuguese government in Malaka and Goa was taken seriously in Batatvia. Believing that a third attack of the Mataram forces was imminent the V.O.C. government sent a squadron of ships to destroy military stores in the Javanese North Coast ports in 1631. No important stores were found, but Japara appeared to be strongly fortified with Portuguese assistance, so the Dutch commander did not storm the town but returned to Batavia without fighting.

p. 178. The V.O.C. government, to some degree reassured as to the king's intentions, decided in 1632 to open preliminaries by sending an envoy with presents to Japara. This initiative led to nothing because of mutual misunderstanding and distrust. The Dutch commander was forced to leave 24 Dutchmen in prison in Japara when he sailed back to Batavia.

p. 185. The capture of the Dutchmen in Japara and the refusal to release them deepened Batavia's distrust. No V.O.C. officials of standing could be found who were willing to re-open negotiations for peace in Tĕgal, as was proposed, in 1634. The ruler of Cĕrbon, a Mataram vassal, tried in vain to mediate. In 1633 the V.O.C. government saw an opportunity to approach the Déwa Agung of Gèlgèl, Mataram's enemy, about an attack on East Java, but the Balinese ruler was not in a position to begin hostilities overseas.

p. 188. The Mataram Court realized that the V.O.C. power could be attacked at sea. So between 1630 and '34 it promoted all kinds of privateering in small craft along the north coast, which brought heavy losses not only to V.O.C. trade, but in greater measure to that of private Chinese and foreign Indonesian traders. The king was expecting the promised support from Malaka in those years. He lost interest in the privateering ventures when it became clear in 1635 that the Portuguese government was unable to send the promised fleet of war-ships to attack Batavia.

Chpt. 11. *Troubles in the interior of the Mataram kingdom after the unsuccessful attacks on Batavia, 1628-'35*

p. 193. The Sundanese rulers of the mountainous Priangan districts of the West Javanese interior had been converted to Islam by the spiritual lord of Gunung Jati and his descendants, the kings of Cĕrbon, in the second half of the 16th century. The Sundanese followed their spiritual leader in acknowledging the suzerainty of Mataram during the reign of Sultan Agung. On the king's order Sundanese forces from Sumĕḍang and Ukur took part in the first siege of Batavia in 1628. Surprised in their camp by a sally of V.O.C. soldiers, they fled to the mountainous district of Sumĕḍang and migrated from there with their families and belongings westward into the territory of the king of Bantĕn, wishing not to be involved in the politics of the lowlands. But they found it impossible to settle either in Bantĕn or in the area of Batavia because of mutual distrust between the migrating mountaineers, speaking an unintelligible idiom, and the Bantĕn and Dutch officials.

p. 195. The Mataram king considered the Sundanese to be deserters and sent troops to punish them in 1630, but the attack was repulsed. In 1632 the Sundanese power was finally crushed by Mataram and Cĕrbon forces which marched on Ukur and Sumĕḍang from the south, east and north simultaneously. Numerous Sundanese prisoners were massacred. The Mataram Court planned a forced migration of Javanese peasants to strategically-located areas in the north-eastern part of the Priangan region.

p. 197. Religiously minded groups in Mataram who adhered to the mystical tradition of the sunan of Tĕmbayat, the legendary apostle of Islam in the southern districts of Central Java, caused some trouble in the country-side around the ancient borough of Wĕḍi in 1630, but the Mataram Court managed to maintain its authority. The malcontents of Wĕḍi were supported by a collateral branch of the royal family, the Tĕpasana clan, who were related to the locally-important Kajoran family, which was to cause much trouble during the reign of Sultan Agung's successor Mangku Rat.

p. 200. The king's pilgrimage to Tĕmbayat, and his erection of an ornamental gate for the grave site, in 1633, marked an intensification of his religious feeling.

p. 204. In the same year, 1633, the Javano-Islamic chronology (A.J.) was made official. Like the pre-Islamic Śaka era it begins in A.D. 78, but employs (Islamic) lunar years after A.J. 1555 (A.D. 1633).

Chpt. 12. *The war with Giri and the end of the independence of the spiritual lords, 1635-'36*

p. 205. Sunan Prapèn, the great ruler of Giri and Grĕsik in the second half of the 16th century, had been succeeded by less fortunate spiritual lords. Nevertheless the authority of the "Raja Bukit" in the Moluccos was still considerable.

p. 209. After the fall of Surabaya in 1625, the surviving prince of the ruling family, called pangéran Pĕkik, was forced to live in Mataram. As a member of one of the oldest East Javanese royal houses he had a considerable civilizing influence at the inland Mataram Court.

p. 213. Pangéran Pekik, married with a sister of Sultan Agung, was made commander of the Surabaya troops which were ordered by the king to subdue the independent ruler of Giri. The Chinese Muslim captain of the Giri forces was killed in battle and the fortified town was taken about 1636.

p. 218. The defeated panĕmbahan Kawis Guwa of Giri was not killed but rather forced to live in Mataram, where he soon died. His heir acknowledged the Mataram suzerainty and was allowed to return as a vassal ruler to Giri.

p. 220. Panĕmbahan Ratu of Cĕrbon, the head of the family of Sultan Agung's principal queen, paid a state visit to Mataram in 1636, probably on the occasion of a family-feast. The presence of the spiritual lords of both Giri and Cĕrbon at his court enhanced Sultan Agung's authority as an Islamic ruler.

Chpt. 13.   *Later relations between the Mataram Court and the Portuguese government in Malaka and Goa, 1634-'40*

p. 223. Portuguese envoys from Malaka again arrived in Mataram in 1636 with valuable presents and promises of support in the war against Batavia from the viceroy in Goa. The king openly revealed his scepticism about the Portuguese promises. The bronze bell offered by the viceroy as a present still exists.

p. 226. Exchange of envoys between Mataram and Malaka/Goa continued from 1638 to 1640. The Portuguese government sent valuable presents, including cannon, in the hope of preventing a rapprochement between the king and the Dutch. Portuguese traders were allowed to settle in Javanese trading-towns where V.O.C. trade was prohibited. Some Portuguese settlements in Javanese towns survived the fall of Malaka to the V.O.C. in 1640-'41..

p. 230. Dominican fathers founded a chapel in Japara for the use of the Portuguese there in 1638. In 1676 the Portuguese fled to Bantĕn during the terrible Truna Jaya war.

Chpt. 14. *Later relations between the Mataram Court and the*
V.O.C. government in Batavia, 1636-'42

p. 233. Throughout the whole period of hostility towards the V.O.C.,
from 1618 until the death of Sultan Agung and even for some years
thereafter, there were Dutch prisoners in Mataram who were kept in
military posts on the highways leading to the capital. Some were
shipwrecked sailors, but others were V.O.C. servants of some standing.
Those who consented to be circumcised and to embrace Islam had
some freedom to move about and married Javanese women. But many
refused to be converted. The prisoners were largely dependent upon
their own resources for their livelihood. The ingenious among them
became petty traders and artisans. They kept up a correspondence with
the V.O.C. government through the intermediary of the Mataram
governor of Tĕgal, who entertained friendly relations with Batavia. This
was not unknown at Court. The V.O.C. sent the prisoners goods to
trade and benefited from the information about Mataram affairs in
their letters. Whenever the relations between Mataram and the V.O.C.
deteriorated the prisoners' lives were in danger. The crownprince, later
sunan Mangku Rat I, entertained friendly relations with some prisoners
in his youth, and thus became more acquainted with the Dutch
mentality than his father ever was.

p. 237. The Batavia government was sincerely concerned about the
condition of the prisoners. Antonio Paulo, a V.O.C. official with the
rank of junior merchant ("onderkoopman"), and a pious man, lived in
Mataram from 1632 to 1642 and acquired a good knowledge of Javanese. He was the acknowledged head of the prisoners' community, and
in some degree was respected by the Javanese officials.

p. 239. In 1636 an energetic second mate of a V.O.C. ship, Abraham
Verhulst, escaped from captivity in an open proa with some companions.
From the mouth of the river Bagawanta on the South Coast they sailed
westward to Bantĕn, where they were helped by the principal of the
British trading-post.

p. 241. Having lost all hope of Portuguese support in the war with
Batavia, Sultan Agung nevertheless saw fit to prolong the negotiations
for peace with the V.O.C. from year to year up to 1642. During this
time he benefited from the valuable presents, including diamonds, which
he received both from the Portuguese and from the V.O.C. He refused
to release the prisoners before having seen a highly qualified V.O.C.
envoy who would humbly sue for peace. The V.O.C. government would

not agree to such a demand. The negotiations by letter were broken off in 1642 after the incident of the British ship Reformation.

Chpt. 15.   *Troubles at the Mataram Court in connection with the crownprince, 1637*

p. 247. The crownprince, later sunan Mangku Rat I, was born about 1619 from a princess of the Cĕrbon family and was married to a daughter of pangéran Pĕkik, the last scion of the House of Surabaya, in 1634. The V.O.C. envoy Rijcklof van Goens, whose reports of his five embassies to the Mataram Court from 1648 to 1654 contain much valuable information, was his contemporary and knew him well.

p. 249. In 1637 and 1638 the Mataram Court was disturbed by a love-affair between the crownprince and a lady from the zenana of his mentor and teacher tumĕnggung Wira Guna, and by the dismissal of two important officers of state who were suspected of plotting against the king's life. Sultan Agung's prompt actions prevented great difficulties.

Chpt. 16.   *The Blambangan war, 1636-'40*

p. 254. The powerful Balinese king (Déwa Agung) of Gèlgèl was acknowledged as suzerain by the Javanese rulers of Blambangan and Panarukan in Java's Eastern Corner from 1616, the year of the Mataram conquest of Pasuruhan, and 1625, when Surabaya fell. The Islamic rulers of Pasuruhan and Surabaya had counter-balanced the "heathen" Balinese influence in the far east of Java before that time. The Blambangan and Panarukan rulers were afraid of an attack from Mataram and approached the V.O.C. government for help. The Déwa Agung did not agree to a V.O.C. suggestion made in 1633 to attack the Mataram vassals in East Java, because he did not have sufficient shipping at his disposal.

p. 256. After an initial success an attack by Mataram on the town of Blambangan was repulsed by Balinese troops which crossed the straits just in time in 1635. These facts are mentioned both in Dutch reports and in Balinese historical literature.

p. 260. Troubles at his Court prevented Sultan Agung from taking further action immediately, but in 1639 a powerful expeditionary force supported by ships was sent to the Eastern Corner. It subdued all the principalities up to Blambangan. The Javanese commanders then planned an attack on Bali, but this did not succeed. The Déwa Agung was nevertheless alarmed and asked the V.O.C. for help. The Dutch response was halfhearted. In any case, Balinese penetration into the Eastern Corner districts was stopped for a time.

p.262. The prisoners of war from East Java and the Eastern Corner were marched to Mataram to work for the king. Their descendants were afterwards called Pinggir and Gajah Mati people.

Chpt. 17. *The king of Mataram's efforts to obtain the title of Sultan, 1641-'42*

p. 264. The Islamic title of Sultan was conferred by the Grand Sherif of Mecca upon the king of Bantěn in 1638. Jealous of his rival in West Java, the king of Mataram sent an envoy to Mecca in 1641 to beg for the same title, and obtained it in return for valuable presents. The Javanese envoy was brought to Surat in a British ship and proceeded from there to Jedda in a Muslim vessel. The voyage was arranged by British factors, who were allowed to stay on in their trading-post in Japara almost without interruption from 1618 to 1652.

p. 268. The Sultan was proud of his new title and sent a party of Javanese men of religion to Mecca, provided with considerable funds, to perform the pilgrimage on his behalf. Although the V.O.C. government offered passage for the party, the Sultan preferred the British ship the Reformation. But the V.O.C. by this time felt strong enough to put a stop to British intrigues at the Mataram Court and intercepted the Reformation as she passed Batavia. Many of the Javanese on board ran amuck and were killed by Dutch marines or by the British crew. One who survived was sent back to Mataram to ask for the release of the Dutch prisoners in return for the passage of the Javanese mission to Surat.

p. 281. Sultan Agung was furious at this interference with his pilgrimage by proxy, and at the loss of face in the eyes of the Meccan Court. In 1642 the Sultan condemned Antonio Paulo, the head of the Dutch prisoners in Mataram, to be thrown to the crocodiles. He was accused of sorcery by which he had warned the V.O.C. government to look out for the Sultan's mission in the British ship. The failure of the British captain to bring the Javanese party safely to Surat caused the British factors and traders to lose the Sultan's favour after 1642.

p. 273. Feeling that he had now achieved all that was possible, the Sultan ordered a comprehensive chronicle of his reign to be written between 1641 and '45. This chronicle is incorported in the great History of Java which was written in the second half of the 18th century.

Chpt. 18. *Relations between the Mataram Court and rulers of other Indonesian states*

p. 274. The V.O.C. fleet of European-built heavy ships could not supersede the Javanese fleets of small craft. Mataram had sufficient shipping of small tonnage, especially after the annexations of Surabaya and Madura, to maintain its position as a maritime power at least on the coasts of Sumatra, Borneo and Celebes. Palémbang's relations with its neighbour of Bantĕn were not good, and this was one incentive for Palémbang to acknowledge the suzerainty of the Central Javanese Mataram king. After the conquest of Malaka in 1641, the V.O.C. felt strong enough to take action against Javanese ships in the Palémbang river. Nevertheless the Palémbang ruler continued to send envoys to Mataram as long as Sultan Agung lived.

p. 277. The Court of Jambi, which as a rule imitated the more powerful rulers of Palémbang, was also faithful in its vassalage to Mataram.

p. 278. The Court of Bañjar Masin had acknowledged the Sultan of Dĕmak as suzerain in the first half of the 16th century. In the first decades of the 17th century the kings of Tuban and Aros Baya (West Madura) contended for suzerainty over Bañjar. Mataram influence became paramount after 1637, and in 1641 the Bañjar Masin ruler sent envoys to Mataram as an obedient vassal.

p. 281. The South Celebes rulers maintained friendly relations with the Mataram Court and supported native headmen in the Moluccos who opposed the monopolistic rule of the V.O.C.

p. 282. Even the Sultan of Bantĕn sent envoys to Mataram in 1642, acknowledging his rival's new title of Sultan.

p. 283. Sultan Agung respected the panĕmbahan Ratu of Cĕrbon as a man of religion and head of his queen's family. He imitated Cĕrbon Court architecture. Meanwhile he urged war with Bantĕn upon the weak state, and requested its support against Batavia. The Cĕrbon rulers were good politicians. As soon as the Mataram kingdom began to totter they accepted the protection of the powerful V.O.C. government in Batavia.

Chpt. 19. *The last years of the reign of Sultan Agung, his death and his burial-place*

p. 284. Although the king refused to make peace, trade between Batavia and the Javanese ports flourished during the last years of his reign. In this period tuměnggung Wira Guna was the most important personage at the Mataram Court and was often mentioned in Dutch reports.

p. 288. Sultan Agung's predecessors were buried beside the mosque in Kuṭa Gěḍé, the old capital of Mataram. The king began to build a new burial-place on a hill nearby about 1631, which became the well-known royal grave-site Imagiri. He was the first king to be buried there.

p. 291. He died in his royal residence in the first half of February, 1646. He had made arrangements for the succession of the crownprince, which was not contested.

IVa.

THE REIGN OF SUNAN MANGKU RAT I, SEDA-ING-TEGAL WANGI, KING OF MATARAM 1646-1677

PART I: THE DISINTEGRATION OF THE REALM

Summary of:

H. J. de Graaf, De regering van Sunan Mangku-Rat I Tegal-Wangi, vorst van Mataram, 1646-1677. I. De ontbinding van het rijk. 's-Gravenhage 1961. *Verhandelingen van het Koninklijk Instituut voor Taal-, Land- en Volkenkunde.* Vol. 33. (This volume contains a description of Mangku Rat's foreign policy, in particular his relations with the V.O.C. in Japara and Batavia).

IVa. SUNAN MANGKU RAT I - PART I

Chpt. 1. *Sunan Mangku Rat's youth and his accession to the throne*

p. 1. The new king was born about 1619. His mother, Ratu Kulon, was the second queen of Sultan Agung (after the repudiation of the first one) and belonged to the family of the rulers of Cěrbon and Batang in West Java, who were related to the revered sunan Gunung Jati, one of the legendary nine saints of Javanese Islam. The name Mangku Rat Agung, by which he is known in history, was given him by Javanese historians after his death, as was his posthumous name Séda-ing-Těgal Wangi (after the place where he was buried). He was married in 1643 to a daughter of pangéran Pěkik, the last prince of Surabaya, who had been forced to live in Mataram since 1625.

p. 3. He was designated to succeed to the throne notwithstanding some youthful aberrations, and at Sultan Agung's death in 1646 he was inaugurated as Susuhunan Ingalaga Mataram. Ample information on his reign is provided by reports of the V.O.C. envoys who were sent regularly by the government in Batavia/Jakarta to visit the Mataram Court. They used to sail to Japara, the beginning of the inland route. The reports written by Rijcklof van Goens are particularly valuable.

p. 4. Tuměnggung Wira Guna, one of the principal officials at the Mataram Court during the last years of the reign of Sultan Agung, supported the new king's accession to the throne.

p. 5. So did the new king's uncle, pangéran Purbaya, a younger brother of Sultan Agung's, although he may have done so reluctantly. The title pangéran Purbaya (= Madyun) was usually given to the brother closest in age (elder or younger) to the sovereign.

p. 8. The Islamic title of Sultan was not hereditary. Mangku Rat never took the trouble to solicit the title from the Sherif of Mecca, although his contemporary the ruler of Bantěn did so in 1651.

Chpt. 2. *The royal residence at Plèrèd and the principal officials*

p. 10. The construction of a dam or weir (plèrèd) which created an artificial lake was begun in the last years of Sultan Agung's reign. Mangku Rat had his new royal residence built near that lake. Brick and hewn stone were more widely used in the construction of walls and buildings than in neighbouring Karta, Sultan Agung's residence, which was built mainly of wood. Karta was abandoned and fell into decay.

p. 14. Tuměnggung Wira Guna, who was made grandvizier (patih) with the title Tuměnggung Mataram in 1646, fell into disgrace soon afterwards. He was an intelligent man and tried to entertain friendly relations with the Dutchmen he met. The administration of the principal inland districts of the realm (Mataram and Pajang) and the outlying provinces on the North Coast was repeatedly altered during Mangku Rat's reign. Officials rarely lasted more than a few years. This bewildered Dutch contemporaries. The centralized organization of the realm sketched in van Goen's reports was never completely put into practice.

p. 20. Beside civil administrators Mangku Rat had tax collectors, who were called treasurers by Dutch observers. Their duties brought them in frequent contact with foreign traders. They were in charge of the royal treasure-house (gěḍong).

Chpt. 3. *The first years of Mangku Rat's reign, 1646-'47*

p. 23. Information provided by Dutch contemporaries and Javanese books written long afterwards do not agree on the events at the beginning of the reign. It is likely that the king had a grudge against the vizier Wira Guna who had been his master in his youth. Mangku Rat made him commander of a campaign against Balinese invaders in Blambangan, in Java's Eastern Corner, where the local ruler Tawang Alun had rebelled. The campaign was not wholly successful and Tawang Alun escaped to Bali. On the way back to Mataram, Wira Guna and some other high officials died as the king had hoped.

p. 27. Mangku Rat had one younger brother born from the same mother. This young prince, called pangéran Alit in history, attempted an ill-advised coup in the capital in the first year of the reign, during the Blambangan campaign when many military men were absent. He ran amuck in the interior of the royal residence. After having killed many prominent noblemen, he died of his wounds and the rebellion was suppressed with much bloodshed. The death of this brother, who might have become a dangerous rival, was a relief to the king.

p. 32. Mangku Rat was convinced of the complicity of a group of Islamic divines and men of religion in pangéran Alit's rebellion. He ordered a massacre and many families of religious people lost their lives, according to van Goens.

p. 34. There is reason to believe van Goens' story that after pangéran Alit's death the queen-mother reconciled Mangku Rat and his uncle

pangéran Purbaya, who had begun to doubt the wisdom of the king's
policy.

p. 36. Mangku Rat considered himself to be the paramount king
of Java and Madura and of the countries in Sumatra, Borneo and
Celebes which had acknowledged the authority of his father Sultan
Agung. In fact the political power of Mataram was dwindling, largely
because Mangku Rat, who was always afraid of rebellions in his capital,
trusted neither his courtiers nor his army and could not adopt a strong
policy in the outlying provinces of the realm.

Chpt. 4.   *The relations between Mataram and Bantĕn,*
           and Mataram and Bali, 1646-'52

p. 39. Panĕmbahan Ratu of Cĕrbon (died 1640) and his son panĕmbahan Giri Laya, descendants of the holy sunan Gunung Jati,
acknowledged the Mataram kings as suzerains. Panĕmbahan Giri Laya
consented to mediate between Bantĕn and Mataram. He even went
so far as to send an expedition by sea to Bantĕn to vindicate an old
claim, but his men were defeated (1650).

p. 42. Mangku Rat was persuaded by Islamic divines to abandon
his plan to attack the Muslim king of Bantĕn in 1652. Relations were
relatively friendly for some years thereafter.

p. 44. Hostilities began again in 1657. Bantĕn traders calling at
Central Javanese ports were molested, and a fleet set out for Bantĕn
from Juwana and Japara. But the ships did not reach Bantĕn; off
Krawang the commanders decided to sail home. The campaign of the
Mataram land-forces was also unsuccessful. The V.O.C. territory around
Batavia/Jakarta, where a strict neutrality was maintained, provided
a buffer between the hostile parties. Peace was restored in 1659.

p. 50. After the unsuccessful campaign against Tawang Alun, the
ruler of Blanmbangan who went over to the side of the Balinese king
in 1646, Mangku Rat made many plans to attack Bali by sea but
nothing came of them. In the meantime, Balinese raiders in the Eastern
Corner of Java destroyed the authority of the Mataram king from
Blambangan to Pasuruhan. Gusti Pañji Sakti, a Balinese adventurer
from Bulèlèng, began his career in the Eastern Corner of Java
about 1664.

Chpt. 5.   *The relations between Mataram and the states in*
           South Sumatra, up to 1659

p. 53. The rulers of Palémbang and Jambi, having acknowledged

the suzerainity of Sultan Agung in his time, continued to pay homage
to Mangku Rat by appearing in person at Court or by sending envoys
up to 1656.

p. 54. V.O.C. trade with Palémbang was carried on by ships which
were sent there regularly from Batavia. The V.O.C. did not have a
fortified trading-post on land. The behaviour of the Dutchmen who
were sent to Palémbang caused such dissatisfaction that a ship lying at
anchor in the river was taken treacherously in 1658. The captain, who
was particularly disliked, and most of the crew were killed or made
prisoner. The rest escaped to Jambi in a boat.

p. 57. Seeing that it was impossible to come to an understanding
with the Palémbang ruler merely by blockading the river, the V.O.C.
government sent a fleet and a detachment of soldiers. The town was
stormed and ransacked and the Court fled to the woods at the end
of 1659. The Dutch prisoners were found crissed. Eventually the V.O.C.
troops left the town and the ruler returned. Mangku Rat had done
nothing in support of his Sumatran vassal.

p. 60. Courtiers and traders whom the new ruler of Palémbang, ki
mas Hindi, who ascended the throne in 1660, sent to do homage in
Mataram were not admitted to the royal presence. The last envoy
returned empty-handed in 1660. Mangku Rat had lost all interest in
overseas states, being preoccupied with difficulties in his own capital.
Ki mas Hindi of Palémbang called himself Sultan Jamaluddin after
1675. He allowed the V.O.C. to establish a trading-post in his town.

p. 64. The ruling family of the neighbouring state of Jambi was
divided. The old ruler adhered to the traditional vassalage to Mataram,
but he was opposed by the crownprince's faction. The Court of Jambi
did not send envoys to Central Java after 1659, and as soon as the new
ruler ascended the throne in 1663 he renounced Mataram suzerainty
and sent envoys to Batavia. The V.O.C. had a trading-post in Jambi
after 1660.

Chpt. 6. *The relations between Mataram and the states in*
         Borneo and Celebes, up to 1659

p. 67. The ruler of Sukadana, in South-West Borneo, was considered
to be a vassal of the Mataram king up to 1656, but after that year he
sided with the Court of Bañjar Masin, in the centre of the South Coast,
which had already renounced Javanese suzerainty. Mangku Rat's
authority in Borneo faded away after 1659.

p. 68. The native traders of Makasar and Gowa, in South Celebes, were rivals of the V.O.C. in the Spice Islands. Portuguese traders who fled from Malaka after it was conquered in 1641 had some influence. Beginning in 1656, South Celebes states sent several times envoys to Mataram to solicit support in their struggle with the V.O.C., but in vain. Mangku Rat refused admittance to Makasarese envoys after 1659. The town of Makasar was stormed and taken by the V.O.C. admiral Speelman in 1669.

Chpt. 7. *The period of friendly relations between the Mataram Court and the V.O.C., 1646-1655.*

p. 74. Sultan Agung of Mataram had been unwilling to make peace with the V.O.C. as long as he lived. Relations became less strained in the last years of his reign, however, and as soon as Mangku Rat became king in 1646 peace was concluded. Among the conditions were that the V.O.C. should send envoys to Mataram annually and that prisoners of war would be exchanged. A number of V.O.C. servants who had been prisoners in Mataram for years had turned Muslim, been circumcised, and had married Javanese women. Dutch envoys were received well and admitted into the royal presence in 1646, 1648 and 1651. Rijcklof van Goens' reports contain interesting information on conditions in the Javanese capital.

Chpt. 8. *The system of two superintendents of the sea-ports of the Mataram kingdom, 1651-1657*

p. 82. Japara had been the principal port of the kingdom of Děmak, and afterwards an independent state, in the 16th century. Annexed by Mataram in the beginning of the 17th century, it continued to function as the gateway to the interior of Central Java until it was superseded by Sěmarang. The first V.O.C. trading-post in Japara, established in 1613, was destroyed by the local Javanese governor in 1617. It was re-established in 1651, in the period of van Goens' good relations with Mangku Rat I. The V.O.C. servants in Japara were considered to be subjects of the king as long as they resided in his territories. He profited by their presence because they supplied him with foreign luxuries.

p. 85. It was difficult to find suitable persons for the office of head of the V.O.C. trading-post at Japara. Some Dutch sailors and V.O.C.

officials who had lived as prisoners in Mataram for many years had learned enough Javanese to be useful interpreters and mediators. Some ship-building activity was begun at the Japara trading-post, but the Javanese authorities were insufficiently cooperative.

p. 88. The governors of the Central Javanese trading-towns (Juwana-Paṭi, Japara, Sĕmarang, Kĕndal) were originally free to negotiate with foreign traders calling at their ports, so long as they observed their obligations to the king's patih in Mataram. Mangku Rat began to realize, however, that his governors received more profit from the trade in his ports than he did himself. He therefore appointed two super-intendents over the seaports who resided at Court and controlled the coastal governors and royal revenues. The coastal districts were divided into an eastern and a western territory, as was the custom at the Java-nese courts. The two territories met at Paṭi.

p. 92. The system of the two superintendents was hard on Javanese and foreign traders, both Chinese and Dutch. Junior officials dis-regarded the local governors' authority and extorted fees whereever they saw that some profit was made. Moreover the king's demands for costly presents from the annual V.O.C. embassies grew steadily, as he realized that oversea trade brought great wealth to the participants. The government in Batavia grew dissatisfied with Mangku Rat's ap-parent unwillingness, which was in fact an impotence, to support the V.O.C. in its plans to monopolize trade in the Archipelago.

Chpt. 9. *The first conflict of Mangku Rat with the V.O.C. government, 1655-'56*

p. 100. Rijcklof van Goens, whose personal relations with the king had been friendly, returned to the Netherlands in 1655. The next V.O.C. envoy was unable to cope with the growing difficulties. Mangku Rat believed that he was being swindled by both the native and foreign traders and ordered all seaports in his realm to be closed in 1655.

p. 103. All traders were inconvenienced by this action. The closing of the ports had been urged by Muslim fanatics who saw the impotence of the Islamic states of Bantĕn and Makasar in resisting the growing power of the infidel V.O.C. There were rumours of war against the V.O.C. in Mataram, but nothing came of it.

Chpt. 10.   *The system of four superior governors of the Central Javanese sea-port, 1657-'60.*

p. 105.   Mangku Rat decided to re-open the seaports in 1657. At the same time the system of the two superintendents residing in Mataram was abrogated. The seaports were divided, not in contiguous territories but mixed-up, among four superior governors who resided in Paṭi, Dĕmak, Japara and Sĕmarang. These officials were expected by the king to monopolize trade with Batavia on his behalf. He delegated all negotiations in matters of trade to them; the king kept aloof. The governors took turns in residing at Court for several months every year. The governor of Paṭi was an intelligent man. He had already visited Batavia in 1653.

p. 114.   This system of a royal monopoly of trade with Batavia was not a success. In 1657 the king prompted the coastal governors to send Javanese trading ships to Malaka and Ambon, in defiance of the V.O.C. monopoly there, and provided them with capital for those ventures. This failed, however, because the V.O.C. refused passports for the ships. Plans to send Javanese traders on Dutch ships to the Coromandel coast also failed. The assistance of British traders, who still had a trading-post in Japara, in carrying Javanese traders to India was of little avail.

p. 119.   Dutch ship-building activity, begun in Japara in 1651, was imitated upon the king's order. Iron was bought in Batavia, and timber was plentiful. Some seagoing vessels of Dutch design were built, but the navigation of them proved too difficult for the Javanese seamen.

p. 120.   Trade between the Japara governor and Makasar was also unsuccessful.

p. 121.   Official V.O.C. envoys were no longer expected in Mataram after 1655. The king wanted his usual presents, however, and the four governors were ordered to supply them regularly. Persian horses, which were needed to improve the native Javanese breed, were selected in Batavia by Javanese experts sent from Mataram.

p. 125.   Finances were the weak point of the Javanese trading activities. The governors borrowed widely in return of vague promises of future supplies of Javanese native produce. The unfulfilled deliveries remained permanently in the V.O.C.'s books. The V.O.C. factors in Japara and the government in Batavia decided to limit the loans. The king and his governors therefore raised the question of customs and duties, from which V.O.C. trade in Japara had been exempt since the establishment of the trading-post. The forceful V.O.C. action in Palémbang and the ransacking of the ruler's residence in that town in 1659 had repercussions in Java. Although Mangku Rat had done nothing in support of his vassal, he suddenly decided in 1660 to close the Javanese ports again to all foreign traders. The king believed that his father-in-law, the aged pangéran Pĕkik of Surabaya, was the head of a conspiracy against his life. The pangéran was killed in 1659. This incident also influenced Mangku Rat's foreign policy.

Chpt. 11. *The second conflict of Mangku Rat with the V.O.C. government, 1660-'61*

p. 134. The V.O.C. was inconvenienced by the closing of the Central Javanese ports and tried to establish a business connection with Surabaya, where the intelligent governor of Paṭi had been recently appointed. This officer was killed upon the king's order in 1660 as a punishment for his friendly relations with the foreigners. The system of the four superior governors of the seaports drew to a close.

p. 143. The governor of Japara stood high in the king's favour for some time. He was active in the Sundanese districts in West Java, where he established Javanese settlements, and in Cĕrbon, where he arranged the administration after the death of the old panĕmbahan who resided in Mataram in 1662. This energetic officer was publicly executed in 1662 because the king was displeased at his business negotiations with Batavia.

Chpt. 12. *The re-established V.O.C. trading-post in Japara, 1661-'66*

p. 150. The king reluctantly realized that trade with the foreigners was indispensable and ordered the Japara trading-post to be given back to the V.O.C. traders in 1661. It was some years before the buildings were again fit for occupation. Mangku Rat again expected a V.O.C. envoy in Mataram, but the Batavia government grew increasingly self-confident as the king's incompetence became more apparent and turned a deaf ear to this suggestion. The Mataram king's authority in East Java also dwindled after 1663.

p. 159. The royal trading monopoly which Mangku Rat had established, hoping to increase his revenue, fell into disuse as the four superior governors lost their power after 1664. The V.O.C. factors in Japara, as they grew familiar with local circumstances, found it advantageous to deal with private merchants, who were mostly Muslims of Indian extraction and Chinese. Their authority in the town superseded that of those Javanese officials who were lower in rank than governor.

Chpt. 13.   *The period of the merchants and the royal government*
            sharing control of the port and town of Japara, 1666-1670

p. 162.   A new governor was appointed in Japara in 1666. He had
to reckon with the influential merchants in town throughout his period
in office. He had some success in arranging the sending of V.O.C.
envoys from Batavia to the Mataram Court in 1667, '68 and '69, the
first embassies since 1655, and he did his best to re-establish friendly
relations. But the V.O.C. did not have a man like Rijcklof van Goens.
Meanwhile V.O.C. trade with all Javanese ports, including those in
East Java, increased in volume and value. Realizing this, the king
availed himself of the opportunity of the annual embassies to increase
his demands for presents, which he considered to be his due. Upon
admittance into the royal presence the Dutchmen were obliged to
behave like vassals offering tribute, sitting on the ground in the open
at a considerable distance from the throne.

p. 181.   The V.O.C. envoy of 1669 was not admitted into the royal
presence. This was because of circumstances in the capital, where royal
authority was dwindling. Mangku Rat quarrelled with his son the crownprince and with important officials. Admiral Speelman's conquest of
the town of Makasar in 1669, the second V.O.C. victory after the
Palémbang war in 1659, bewildered the Javanese Court. An energetic
governor of Japara, who was considered overbearing, was killed upon
the king's order in 1672. Relations among the Mataram Court, the
governors in the coastal provinces and the V.O.C. government in
Batavia became chaotic as a result of the unpredictable measures of
Mangku Rat, who distrusted everybody.

Chpt. 14.   *The period of the wardens of the ports (shahbandar) side by*
            side with territorial administrators (umbul), 1670-1677

p. 192.   Realizing that trade was ever more important as a source of
revenue, the king appointed wardens of the ports to negotiate with
foreign traders and to collect the duties. No new governors were
appointed, and the duties of those in function were changed into war-
denships. The umbuls, originally heads of inland districts under the
control of the governors, were given greater authority in the country
than before. It was the king's scheme that wardens and umbuls should
balance each other. The result was anarchy.

p. 195.   The shahbandar of Japara was a man of business who was engaged in trade in many places. He had dealings with important personages at Court including the crownprince, with Chinese merchants (some of them converted Muslims) in Japara and Batavia, and with the V.O.C. He was accused of dishonesty and extortionate practices and dismissed in 1675. His onerous taxation had caused V.O.C. trade to move from Japara to Sĕmarang, which had closer connections with the interior. New troubles in East Java with Makasarese and Madurese raiders so distracted the king's attention that he ignored difficulties in the neighbouring coastal districts of Central Java during the last years of his reign.

pp. 207-212 contain a short Dutch summary, and a bibliography.

IVb.

THE REIGN OF SUNAN MANGKU RAT I, SEDA-ING-TEGAL WANGI, KING OF MATARAM 1646-1677

PART II: INSURRECTION AND DOWNFALL

Summary of:

H. J. de Graaf, De regering van Sunan Mangku-Rat I Tegal-Wangi, vorst van Mataram, 1646-1677. II. Opstand en ondergang. 's-Gravenhage 1962. *Verhandelingen van het Koninklijk Instituut voor Taal-, Land- en Volkenkunde.* Vol. 39. (This volume contains a description of developments at the Mataram Court and in the interior of the kingdom which led to Mangku Rat's abandonment of his capital).

IVb. SUNAN MANGKU RAT I - PART II

Chpt. 1.   *The crownprince (later sunan Mangku Rat II),*
his youth up to 1659

p. 1.   Mangku Rat I was married in 1643 to a daughter of pangéran
Pĕkik, the last Surabaya prince who was forced to live at the Mataram
court. This first queen died soon after the birth of her third child, who
was designated crownprince. Proposals to marry him to princesses from
the Bantĕn or Cĕrbon royal families came to nothing. The crownprince's
disorderly life increased his father's difficulties at home.

p. 4.   In 1659, about ten years after the death of his first queen,
Mangku Rat I was led to believe that his father-in-law pangéran Pĕkik
was the head of a conspiracy against his life. The pangéran was killed
upon the king's order with all his relatives, including those residing in
Surabaya. The Surabaya family was one of the last to survive, and
certainly the most important, of the old royal Houses which had reigned
in East Java before Sultan Agung annexed those districts by force.
Mangku Rat's distrust of all noblemen and prominent persons in
Mataram demanded numerous victims during the following years.

Chpt. 2.   *The period of the conspiracies of the princes:*
the crownprince and pangéran Purbaya, 1660-1670

p. 10.   The massacre of the Surabaya family was the beginning of
the discord which divided the House of Mataram. The crownprince
had loved his maternal grandfather, and therefore nursed a grudge
against his father; Mangku Rat I likewise distrusted his son as long
as he lived.

p. 13.   Collateral branches of the Mataram family were rebellious,
and several noblemen were killed at the king's order after 1660.

p. 15.   An infatuation of Mangku Rat for a beautiful woman who
did not belong to the Mataram nobility caused a great commotion at
Court. She is known in history as Ratu Malang. She was the king's
favourite until her death (perhaps by poison) in 1667.

p. 22.   A love-affair between the crownprince and a girl intended as
Ratu Malang's successor divided father and son still more. The girl,
known as rara Oyi, was killed at the king's order in 1667.

p. 26. Pangéran Purbaya, the king's uncle, was compromised and some of his relatives fell victims to Mangku Rat's distrust. The crownprince sided with the rebellious princes.

Chpt. 3. *The period of the crownprince's disgrace, 1670-1672*

p. 31. The crownprince had a love-affair with Ratu Blitar, the wife of his half-brother pangéran Singasari. This produced a scandal which led the king to banish the crownprince from Court for some time. The young man set out on a journey during which he visited the Dutch trading-post at Japara and established relations with the V.O.C. In 1670 he returned to Mataram. The king gave him the East Javanese district of Surabaya as an appanage at this time. The crownprince resided in Mataram and had a steward in Surabaya to collect his revenue.

Chpt. 4. *The beginning of the rapprochement between the crownprince and radèn Kajoran*

p. 38. Kajoran, an ancient site south of the town of Klatèn, was the seat of an illustrious family of men of religion. They were descendants of a brother of sunan Těmbayat, the holy man from Sěmarang who had been one of the first to spread knowledge of Islam in the inland districts of Central Java in the first half of the 16th century. The Kajoran family and the House of Mataram had been related by marriage for four generations. The head of the family, alarmed at the massacre of noblemen at Court by Mangku Rat, sympathized with the crownprince in his difficulties.

Chpt. 5. *The beginning of the good understanding between the crownprince and radèn Truna Jaya, 1670*

p. 46. Radèn Truna Jaya was a descendant of the last king of West Madura (Bangkalan and Sampang) who was forced to live in Mataram after the annexation of his country by Sultan Agung. Jealousy among the Madurese princes living in Mataram led radèn Truna Jaya to leave the Court at Plèrèd and move to Kajoran, where he married a daughter of the head of the family.

p. 51. Radèn Kajoran promoted an understanding between his son-in-law who felt slighted and the crownprince who nursed a grudge against his father.

Chpt. 6.   *The beginning of Truna Jaya's rule in Madura, 1670-1671*

p. 54.   Standing high in the crownprince's favour, Truna Jaya was allowed to leave Mataram and to return to Madura. He appealed to Madurese allegiance to his own family and to the House of Surabaya, of which his patron the crownprince was a descendant, and won a great number of followers among the local gentry. The authority of his rival the pangéran of Sampang, who still resided in Mataram, dwindled, and after some fighting Truna Jaya became master of Madura.

Chpt. 7.   *The Makasarese refugees and pirates in Java, 1670-1674*

p. 62.   After Makasar, the principal eastern trading-centre outside Java, was stormed and taken by the V.O.C. admiral Cornelis Speelman in 1669, bands of Makasarese soldiers and adventurers headed by members of noble families sought their fortunes overseas in piracy and war. This had been the practice in South Celebes from olden times. An Islamic divine from Makasar, known as sèh Yusup, lived in Bantĕn after about 1670. He had considerable influence at Court and promoted the admittance to Bantĕn of a group of Makasarese refugees led by a noblemen called kraèng Bonto Marannu.

p. 66.   The relations between the Bantĕn Court and the unruly Makasarese guests became strained after some time. The Makasarese were forced to leave in 1674. They sailed eastward and became pirates, harassing the North Coast trading-towns. At last, having come to an understanding with the crownprince of Mataram, they were permitted to settle in Dĕmung, a remote district in the Eastern Corner of Java (Bĕsuki).

p. 70.   Another group of Makasarese refugees, headed by the kraèng of Galésong, engaged in piracy along the coasts of the eastern islands, in particular Sumbawa. Then they came to East Java in 1675.

Chpt. 8.   *The V.O.C. government chasing the Makasarese pirates*

p. 73.   An action of a small V.O.C. fleet on the coasts of the eastern islands caused another group of warlike Makasarese refugees led by daèng Manggappa to move to Bantĕn in 1674. They made themselves a nuisance, as had their predecessors, and were forced to leave for East Java in 1675.

p. 77.   A severe famine caused by crop failure prevailed in Central Java from 1674-1676. This calamity and the king's bad health paralysed Mataram political activity in those years.

Chpt. 9. *The first raids of Makasarese bands on Javanese towns*

p. 81. A raid by Makasarese pirates from Děmung on Grěsik was
repulsed in 1674. The V.O.C. authorities in Batavia suspected that
several local Javanese officials who were partisans of the crownprince
had connived at the attack on the king's territory. Mangku Rat made
plans to maintain his rights, but nothing came of it. The king's authority
in the capital was balanced by the crownprince's.

p. 84. The Makasarese headmen in East Java planned a second
raid in 1675. The kraeng of Galésong and Truna Jaya, ruler of Madura,
entered into a pact, sealed by intermarriage, to raid the prosperous
trading-towns of the North Coast provinces. Supported by Madurese
power, the Makasarese raiders took and burned the principal towns
from Pajarakan in the Eastern Corner to Surabaya and Grěsik. The
resistance offered by some loyal Mataram officers was of no avail. The
inhabitants of the towns, fearing a massacre, fled into the interior of
the country.

p. 90. Fearing an imminent Makasarese raid in Central Java in
1676, Mangku Rat sent a military man as governor to Japara to replace
the covetous shahbandar who had made many enemies. The town was
reinforced and provided with cannon.

Chpt. 10. *Joint actions of the V.O.C. government and the
king of Mataram against the Makasarese raiders, 1676*

p. 92. A V.O.C. fleet sent from Batavia to fight the Makasarese
forces on the North Coast was at first met with distrust by the loyal
Mataram officers. Communication and cooperation were difficult. A
Mataram force marching on Děmung was defeated, and combined
actions by V.O.C. and Mataram ships on the coast of the Eastern
Corner were not always successful. Nevertheless the kraeng of Galésong
decided to leave Děmung. He joined his ally Truna Jaya in Madura.

p. 110. Truna Jaya called himself paněmbahan Madu Rětna (after
his new residence) after 1676. He was supported by the sunan of Giri,
near Grěsik, an influential spiritual authority who represented the
true faith and the old East Javanese patriotism, in opposition to the
Mataram king who was in league with the infidel V.O.C. and had
massacred the rightful East Javanese rulers.

p. 112. A second V.O.C. fleet sent from Batavia to Děmung was
successful. The Makasarese fortifications were destroyed and their ships

were burned. The Dutch commander visited Madura afterwards, but did not take action against Truna Jaya.

Chpt. 11. *The crownprince's treacherous behaviour and the defeat of the Mataram forces, 1676*

p. 115. Mangku Rat sent a considerable number of troops, commanded by the crownprince, to East Java to fight the Makasarese invaders and the Madurese insurgents who had in the meantime crossed the straits of Madura and taken Surabaya. Marching slowly eastward along the north coast, after a long delay in Japara, the Mataram forces and their West Javanese auxiliaries met the enemy in Gěgodog, east of Tuban. The battle ended in the complete defeat of Mangku Rat's army. The aged pangéran Purbaya was slain, the Javanese troops were routed, and the crownprince and his brothers fled to Mataram. The crownprince was blamed for this disaster. He had wavered for a long time before deciding to attack the Madurese and East Javanese forces headed by Truna Jaya, who had been his protégé some years before. There were rumours that he had connived with his father's enemies.

Chpt. 12. *The victory of the Madurese arms*

p. 129. The Madurese bands lost no time after their spectacular victory. The Javanese trading-towns on the North Coast from Surabaya westward were taken and laid in ruin within a few months. Their fortifications had been dismantled after their annexation by Sultan Agung about 50 years before. Only Japara was saved for the king, through the united efforts of the new military governor sent from Mataram in great haste and the V.O.C. servants of the trading-post, reinforced by Dutch soldiers and sailors who arrived by sea from Batavia just in time. The Madurese attack on Japara was beaten off. This rescue considerably enhanced the prestige of the V.O.C. in the Javanese North Coast districts and at the Mataram Court.

p. 133. Leaving Japara alone the Madurese captains, who commanded numerous troops of Javanese hangers-on, all of them eager for booty, and controlled ships taken from the conquered towns, forced the West Javanese coastal districts as far as Cěrbon to acknowledge Truna Jaya's authority. The V.O.C. in Batavia stopped penetration further west. The old towns of Kudus and Děmak, although courageously defended by Mataram troops for some time, were also taken by the Madurese.

p. 135. Relations between Truna Jaya and the Makasarese captains became strained after 1677, because of the arrogance of the foreign pirates and the Madurese prince's desire to establish order in the part of Java which he commanded. There was some fighting in East Java and Madura. The Makasarese settled down after some time, content with what they had got, in the district of Pasuruhan.

Chpt. 13. *The defection of radèn Kajoran from the king's cause, and the troubles in the interior of the realm in 1676*

p. 138. After the victory in the battle of Gĕgodog, Madurese troops pursued the routed Javanese army into the interior of East and Central Java. Marching on Mataram from the east, the Madurese and East Javanese invaders were joined in Taji, the entrance to the district of Mataram, by the men of radèn Kajoran, Truna Jaya's father-in-law and the semi-independent head of a powerful native clan related to the family of religious leaders of Tĕmbayat.

p. 139. The invasion was stopped temporarily by loyal Mataram troops commanded by princes of the blood, but radèn Kajoran escaped and joined Truna Jaya.

p. 142. He continued his action against the Mataram Court, creating commotion in the inland districts east of Mataram where his influence was great.

p. 144. One of the younger Mataram princes, campaigning against the Madurese invaders in the districts west and north of Mataram, had some success in restoring the king's authority in those parts.

Chpt. 14. *The actions of admiral Cornelis Speelman in Japara, in the beginning of 1677*

p. 146. After the battle of Gĕgodog in 1676 the three parties concerned, Truna Jaya, the crownprince and the king's governor in Japara, sent letters to Batavia to beg for V.O.C. help in their difficulties. The V.O.C. government decided to step in. The best man available at the moment was Cornelis Speelman, the victor in the Makasar war of 1669. He sailed with a considerable fleet, an expeditionary force of Europeans and Indonesians and a well-equipped staff of Dutch V.O.C. officials for Japara.

p. 149. The admiral anchored his fleet in the roads and resided with his staff in the town of Japara. He collected information on the

entangled affairs of the Mataram kingdom from all sides, by sending
envoys to Truna Jaya in Surabaya and to the king in Mataram. The
Dutch admiral and the king's governor in Japara came to be on pleasant
terms. Truna Jaya declined an invitation to visit Speelman in Japara
for negotiations. The Madurese and East Javanese forces were still
winning ground in the interior of the country.

p. 152. After a long interchange of envoys between Japara and the
Mataram Court, Mangku Rat, who was seriously ill, and the princes,
in a panic because of the Kajoran and Madurese troubles in the interior
of the country, gave the admiral a general authority to take action
against Truna Jaya and even to negotiate with the Madurese ruler in
the king's name. The V.O.C. obtained promises of payment from the
Mataram Court for the assistance, but the payments could not be made
before Truna Jaya was vanquished. The Javanese military and naval
resources which were put at the admiral's disposal were negligible.

Chpt. 15.   *The actions of admiral Cornelis Speelman in Surabaya
in the middle of 1677*

p. 162. The admiral sailed for Surabaya and anchored there in
April, 1677. He tried to have a personal talk with Truna Jaya on the
state of Java. Although he declared himself to be a friend of the V.O.C.,
the Madurese ruler was distrustful and declined invitations to come into
the fleet. Even an appointment to meet in a boat lying off-shore was
not kept. Truna Jaya was addicted to liquor, and his actions were
unpredictable. He was confident of his army's success in the interior
of East Java, and of radèn Kajoran's influence in Central Java.

p. 167. After a month of unsuccessful negotiating the admiral landed
troops in the outskirts of the town of Surabaya and met with little
resistance. Further negotiations were again unsuccessful. Truna Jaya
was unwilling to acknowledge Mangku Rat's suzerainity in Madura.

p. 170. In order not to lose more valuable time, Speelman stormed
the fortified town of Surabaya with Dutch and Indonesian companies,
among them Makasarese, and took it after some hard fighting. Truna
Jaya escaped and retreated into the interior of East Java. He established
head-quarters in the old capital of Kaḍiri. Dutch captains commanding
Indonesian companies dislodged the Madurese forces from their posi-
tions in the districts near Surabaya.

p. 173. The Makasarese kraèng of Galésong, settled in Pasuruhan,
had quarreled with Truna Jaya and remained neutral during the

conflict in Surabaya. But he did not submit to the admiral as the representative of the Mataram king, after the fall of Surabaya. Speelman employed several foreigners, including Indian traders, as his envoys.

p. 174. The local rulers of Madura, Truna Jaya's native country, were forced by V.O.C. troops to acknowledge the admiral's and the sunan's authority. Truna Jaya's residence in West Madura, Madu Rĕtna, was stormed and laid in ruin. But then the unexpected news of the occupation of the capital of Plèrèd by Madurese and Kajoran forces and the flight of the sunan westward made the admiral decide to sail immediately for Japara, to defend that important strategic point. He left the occupied towns in East Java and Madura with weak Dutch and Indonesian garrisons.

p. 179. Speelman had expected loyal Mataram troops in the interior to profit by the defeat of Truna Jaya in Surabaya. But the Mataram kingdom was disorganized and unable to help itself.

Chpt. 16. *The decisive attack of the Madurese forces on the king's residence of Plèrèd and the capitulation of the Mataram government, in June, 1677*

p. 181. Truna Jaya's captains, commanding Madurese troops and numerous Javanese auxiliaries, campaigned successfully in the interior of East and Central Java. Only a few important towns on the North Coast, such as Japara and Sĕmarang, were saved for the king with the assistance of V.O.C. forces. Radèn Kajoran's influence in the countryside paved the way for the Madurese marching on Mataram from the east. Mangku Rat was grievously ill and nearly demented, the princes distrusted one another, and did not offer any organized resistance, although each of them still had a company of armed body-guards at his disposal. In an atmosphere of anarchy and panic, the aged king left his residence with a small retinue and retreated slowly to the west, the only area not yet infested by the enemy. As soon as the king had left, Madurese and East Javanese regular troops and marauders penetrated into the residential quarters of the capital and entered the royal compound and the compounds of the absent princes and officials. There was almost no fighting, but much fire-raising and plundering. The royal treasury and the women who were taken captive were transported to Kaḍiri. Only the compounds of the Madurese and Cĕrbon princes and that of pangéran Purbaya, who was related to radèn Kajoran, were spared.

Chpt. 17. *Sunan Mangku Rat's retreat westward and his death in Tĕgal, June-July, 1677*

p. 188. The aged king, leaving his residence with a small retinue, was neither pursued nor molested. Grievously ill, he was carried for more than two weeks in a palanquin westward through the districts of Bagĕlèn and the mountainous region of Bañumas. He hoped to reach Tĕgal to meet a V.O.C. official waiting for him there in a ship. Tĕgal is near Batang, whence came the king's mother. On the way he was joined by the crownprince and had time to hand his son the regalia and holy weapons symbolizing royalty, which he had brought from Mataram. Mangku Rat died in a small village before reaching the coast. His body was transported to Tĕgal and buried there on the top of an artificial hill, which gave him his posthumous name Séda-ing-Tĕgal Wangi. The crownprince, although for the time being without any resources, was acknowledged as king of Mataram by the V.O.C. officials in Tĕgal and Japara.

Addenda, *pp. 195-214*: a Dutch bibliography, a Javanese-Dutch glossary of terms used in the text, and an alphabetic register of personal and geographical names.

V.

THE EXPEDITION OF ADMIRAL ANTHONIO HURDT
TO THE INNER PARTS OF JAVA
SEPTEMBER - DECEMBER 1678

Summary of:

H. J. de Graaf (ed.), De expeditie van Anthonio Hurdt, Raad van Indië, als admiraal en superintendent naar de binnenlanden van Java, sept.-dec. 1678, volgens het journaal van Johan Jurgen Briel, secretaris. Met een inleiding en aantekening van —. 's-Gravenhage 1971. *Werken uitgegeven door de Linschoten-Vereeniging.* Vol. LXXII.

V. HURDT'S EXPEDITION TO KADIRI

Introduction on Javanese history, 1677-'78

p. 1. The new king of Mataram, Mangku Rat II, was accepted by the Javanese gentry in Tĕgal (his grandmother's country). He tried without success to establish his authority in Cĕrbon. The governor of Cĕrbon, a steward of the panĕmbahan who had been forced to live as a vassal at the Mataram court since 1660, availed himself of the opportunity to regain independence for the old principality and refused to come to Tĕgal and pay homage. He had the support of the Court of Bantĕn, where the Mataram king's alliance with the infidel V.O.C. government of Batavia was looked on with disfavour. Mangku Rat II was, however, acknowledged as king in Pĕkalongan. He was able to collect a sufficiently strong force of West Pasisir men to march from Pĕkalongan through the Bañumas and Bagĕlèn districts to Mataram, in order to dislodge the Madurese. Truna Jaya intended to make Kaḍiri the capital of a new East Javanese kingdom and was not interested in Mataram, so he had ordered his troops to withdraw eastward with their booty. Pangéran Pugĕr, a younger brother of Mangku Rat II, had been appointed commander-in-chief of the rest of the loyal Mataram troops in the last days of the old king's reign, and had availed himself of the opportunity to occupy the ruins of the royal residence of Plèrèd when they were abandoned by the Madurese. Considering himself to be the rightful king, he called himself susuhunan Ingalaga Mataram and refused admittance to the capital to the new West Pasisir forces sent by his brother. Mangku Rat's captains did not take action; they established a fortified camp on the western border of the Mataram district, and waited to see how things would develop. Realizing his inability to get hold of his inheritance with his own limited resources, Mangku Rat II decided to throw in his fortune unreservedly with the V.O.C. He moved with his family and the small retinue he had collected from Tĕgal to Japara in Dutch ships put at his disposal by admiral Speelman.

p. 13. The admiral had been alarmed by the occupation of the Mataram capital by Truna Jaya's troops and had decided to sail immediately for Japara, leaving Surabaya in charge of a relative of panĕmbahan Agung of Giri (1637-'80) called adipati Tumapĕl. V.O.C.

landing forces recovered the most important towns of the Central Javanese coastal districts, Sĕmarang, Dĕmak, Kudus and Pați, for the king. In concert with Mangku Rat, who had made Japara his residence for the time being, Speelman repeatedly sent envoys to pangéran Pugĕr, who was busy reorganizing the Mataram kingdom in the interior of the country. The admiral invited him, with the other princes, to come to Japara to discuss the state of the realm, but the pangéran refused, on the excuse of the epidemics and famine prevailing in Mataram. Mangku Rat was alone in Japara, unsupported by his brothers and without material resources; he saw himself obliged to accept the admiral's onerous terms for V.O.C. assistance in securing his inheritance and restoring the monarchy. To pay the considerable sums of money requested by the V.O.C. for expenses, the king offered as security the taxes and duties of all harbour-towns on the North Coast from Krawang in the west to Blambangan in the east. Moreover he relinquished his suzerainty, which up to that time had been acknowledged by the V.O.C., over the kingdom of Jakarta, from the Java Sea to the Southern Ocean. He agreed to recognize the sole jurisdiction of V.O.C. courts of justice over all foreigners residing or sojourning in his states, whether Europeans, non-Javanese Indonesians (Makasarese, Malays, Balinese), Chinese, or Indians, etc. These terms, and some mercantile privileges, were couched in commercial contracts. The V.O.C., being an association of merchants, had now engaged in a hazardous speculation; they expected to be paid for their services in the future, when their associate was king of Mataram.

p. 18. After concluding the contracts, Mangku Rat expected a speedy return to Mataram, escorted by the admiral and his troops. Circumstances were unfavourable, however. Tĕgal, Sĕmarang, Japara and Rĕmbang were the only fortified towns on the North Coast where the king's authority was acknowledged. The town of Surabaya was reoccupied by Madurese troops and the fortified V.O.C. trading-post was cut off from the hinterland.

p. 21. The Makasarese kraèng of Galésong, who had quarreled with his father-in-law Truna Jaya, sided with Mangku Rat II and began a campaign from his headquarters in Pasuruhan against the Madurese capital in Kaḍiri. Truna Jaya held his own, however, and the Makasarese captain retreated to a strong position in the delta of the river Brantas upstream from Surabaya. After this incident Truna Jaya decided to concentrate his troops in Kaḍiri. Mataram and Pajang were abandoned. Partisans of radèn Kajoran and followers of pangéran

Pugĕr, who resided in the ruins of the old capital of Mataram, divided the districts in the interior of Central Java.

p. 25. An expeditionary force of loyal Javanese sent from Japara against Kajoran partisans in Paṭi and Jipang was unsuccessful. The commanders quarreled, and one of them, the governor of Tĕgal, proved unreliable. Both were killed. Smaller campaigns by European and Indonesian V.O.C. companies under Dutch commanders, with Javanese auxiliaries, occupied some strategic points in Central Java on the borders of Mataram and Pajang and garrisoned them. Pangéran Pugĕr remained inactive and neutral in Mataram proper. There was some fighting with followers of another Mataram prince, pangéran Marta Sana. The deaths of this prince and his brother pangéran Singasari simplified matters. Henceforth Mangku Rat II and pangéran Pugĕr were the only pretenders to the throne of Mataram.

p. 34. Cornelis Speelman was seriously ill and exhausted after 16 months in command of the V.O.C. forces in Central and East Java. He was ordered to return to Batavia in March, 1678. His reports on the state of the Mataram kingdom persuaded the V.O.C. government that it was necessary to take forceful action in support of Mangku Rat, who was impatient for his installation as king as promised in the contracts. Anthonio Hurdt, former governor of Ambon, was made commander of a considerable force of European and Indonesian V.O.C. troops sent from Batavia to Japara by sea. His instructions were to restore order in Central and East Java by placing Mangku Rat on the throne of the Mataram kingdom.

p. 38. After Speelman's departure from Japara a new enemy of the king and the V.O.C. appeared in the interior of Central Java west of Mataram. He was a Makasarese adventurer called Raja Namrud, a leader of Makasarese and Balinese outlaws who sought connections with the Kajoran partisans. A small V.O.C. garrison in a Mataram border-town had some difficulty in forcing him to retreat to the Bañumas districts. A Madurese campaign from East Java against Japara was stopped just in time by the appearance of the V.O.C. reinforcements commanded by Anthonio Hurdt in the roads of Dĕmak.

The campaign of 1678

p. 40. The new admiral proposed to attack Truna Jaya in Kaḍiri from Surabaya, which was the shortest route. But he was persuaded by Mangku Rat to go the long way through the Pasisir districts of Dĕmak,

Grobogan and Jipang to the Brantas valley, in order to attack Kaḍiri from the west. The king felt that the slow passage of the troops through the inland districts would overawe enemies and the Kajoran partisans who were wavering which side to take, and in the end he was proved to be right. Besides the main column led by the admiral and the king, there were lateral columns led by V.O.C. captains marching from Japara on Kaḍiri, one by a southern route through the districts of Pajang and Madyun, and another by a northern route *via* Paṭi and Rĕmbang. The three columns consisted of regular V.O.C. companies (the minority of whom were European soldiers and marines, the majority Indonesians) all under the command of V.O.C. officers, and Javanese auxiliaries. The auxiliaries grew in number as the campaign proceeded, for bands headed by local leaders joined the king's party, eager for booty.

p. 42. Anthonio Hurdt found the march through unknown districts and the crossing of several rivers very difficult for the V.O.C. forces, and he would have preferred to stay in the valley of the Bĕngawan Sala at Grompol and defer the march on Kaḍiri to the next year. But he was again persuaded by Mangku Rat to continue, notwithstanding heavy losses through illness and food shortages. The countryside was ransacked by the king's men collecting food for the V.O.C. troops, as was stipulated. The villagers fled in panic to the hills. The main column at last reached Singkal, on the west bank of the river Brantas, nearly opposite the town of Kaḍiri. It was joined there by the lateral columns, and also by a train of more than 800 ox-carts laden with victuals for the troops, convoyed all the way up from the Brantas delta by the V.O.C. factor of Surabaya. He had been successful in securing assistance from the Makasarese kraèng of Galésong and the adipati of Tumapĕl, who had held the town of Surabaya for the V.O.C.

p. 45. The taking of the strongly fortified town of Kaḍiri was a matter of time. Crossing the river Brantas offered the greatest difficulty. Nearly two months after the arrival of the troops in Singkal on the west bank of the river, in November, 1678, the town was stormed and taken by a V.O.C. force commanded by captain Tack (the same officer who was killed in Kartasura in 1686) and irregular Javanese auxiliaries. The town was sacked, which gave Truna Jaya time to escape south-ward with a small retinue. Mangku Rat was offered ceremoniously a crown found in Truna Jaya's residence; this crowning ceremony was significant only for the Europeans, for Javanese kings were never "crowned". The Madurese adipati of Sampang, Truna Jaya's kinsman, and his followers and other noblemen who had sided with Truna Jaya, submitted to the king.

p. 47. The fortifications of Kaḍiri were dismantled and the town was left in charge of a loyal governor. The troops proceeded to Surabaya along the river Brantas in proas, on foot and on horseback. Losses from illness and accidents on the river were great. They arrived in Surabaya in the beginning of 1679. Those who had taken part in the campaign needed sorely a period of recuperation. Many died in hospital from sheer exhaustion. Mangku Rat took up residence in the compound of the governor of Surabaya; his mother had been a Surabaya princess and he himself had been appointed viceroy of East Java by his father about 1670. He had brought a small retinue, including some women of standing, from Japara and he was able to establish a small royal Court. The V.O.C. staff officers, among them the admiral, embarked for Batavia soon afterwards. Anthonio Hurdt's successor as commander of the V.O.C. forces in East Java was Christiaan Poleman.

pp. 51-57 contain notes on the Dutch V.O.C. officers who were active in Central and East Java at the time of the campaign of 1678-'79, and their lives.

pp. 58-63 contain notes on the character and position in Javanese history of sunan Mangku Rat II (1677-1703), the king who took the initiative for the alliance between the House of Mataram and the V.O.C. which stood for over a century, and notes on his only son and successor Mangku Rat III (1703-'08) and his brother pangéran Pugĕr, later Paku Buwana I (1703-'19), the ancestor of all Javanese kings after him.

pp. 64-70 contain notes on the Javanese courtiers and officials who served Mangku Rat II in the first years of his reign.

pp. 70-72 contain notes on Truna Jaya and his family, and some notes on the East Javanese ruler of Kĕrtasana (downstream of Kaḍiri on the river Brantas), who remained true to Truna Jaya's cause even after the defeat and became a guerilla leader in Pugĕr (in the Eastern Corner of Java) in alliance with the Balinese adventurer Surapati (1686).

pp. 72-73 contain notes on the original Dutch map which is reproduced in the book.

pp. 76-277 contain the Diary of Johan Jurgen Briel.

pp. 278-288 contain an index of personal and geographical names.

VI.

CAPTURE AND DEATH OF RADEN TRUNA JAYA
DECEMBER 1679 - JANUARY 1680

Summary of:

H. J. de Graaf, Gevangenneming en dood van Raden Truna-Djaja, 26 Dec. 1679 - 2 Jan. 1680. Jakarta 1952. *Tijdschrift voor Indische Taal-, Land- en Volkenkunde* (*T.B.G.*). Vol. 85, pp. 273-309.

VI. RADEN TRUNA JAYA'S DEATH

p. 273. Javanese tales of Truna Jaya's end, incorporated in 18th-century Central Javanese Babads, are romanticized. They are at variance with Dutch reports written by V.O.C. officials who were on the spot. These reports are preserved in the State Archives at The Hague.

p. 274. After the fall of his capital at Kaḍiri, Truna Jaya retreated along the river Brantas upstream, passing the towns of Blitar and Malang. The pursuit by the king's irregular Javanese troops was ineffectual. Truna Jaya still had a small force of devoted Madurese warriors and began to establish a new centre of action in the hilly and sparsely-populated Batu region west of Malang, between the mountains Kawi and Arjuna, which had belonged to great pre-Islamic East Javanese states. He still kept in touch with his adherents in the interior of East Java, including those in Panaraga and Kĕrtasana, and he asked the Sultan of Bantĕn and the ruler of Bulèlèng for help, but in vain. The district of Batu produced insufficient food, and his Madurese followers were decimated by disease.

p. 277. Christiaan Poleman, Hurdt's successor as commander of the V.O.C. forces in East Java, died after a short time and the command was given to Jacob Couper. His first action was directed against the kraèng of Galésong, who had established a fortified centre of Makasarese in Kakapar (or Kèpĕr) in the Brantas delta. The fortification was stormed and taken by a small V.O.C. force with Buginese auxiliaries. But the kraèng escaped to the hills where he died of exhaustion in the residence of his father-in-law Truna Jaya, with whom he had quarreled for a long time. Most of the Makasarese made peace with the V.O.C. captain Jeremias van Vliet; they and their families were sent back to Celebes in V.O.C. ships. So Truna Jaya was deprived of his auxiliaries.

p. 280. After a short period of rest in Surabaya, the king with his retinue and the commander Jacob Couper moved to Kakapar. The commander sent several letters to Truna Jaya in his mountain retreat to persuade him to submit to the king, since his position was hopeless. Truna Jaya did not believe that the V.O.C. forces had come only to fight in the king's service, as the commander said. At last Couper decided to attack. Truna Jaya's fortified residence in Ngantang was stormed and taken with great difficulty, but the leader escaped once more over mountain-passes southward.

p. 284. Buginese warriors who where sent in pursuit returned after a short time empty-handed. There were rumours that they had been bribed to give up the pursuit. Couper distrusted the Buginese as auxiliaries and observed that their leader Aru Palakka did not stand well with the king. So he hastened their return to their native island. Couper was not in a position to pursue Truna Jaya himself as he had fallen ill, so he came down from Ngantang to recuperate in Biara.

p. 287. The king proceeded westward from Kakapar and taking up residence in Payak, a village not far from Biara, he began his own correspondence with Truna Jaya without the commander's knowledge, to invite the rebel to submit. In his answer Truna Jaya tried to persuade the king to break away from the V.O.C. alliance and to restore the old kingdom of Majapahit, the capital of which had not been far away. The king did not respond to this suggestion, but took the initiative and ordered the Ambonese V.O.C. captain Jonker with his men to find Truna Jaya in the highlands and to bring him down a captive.

p. 292. Jacob Couper, although still ill, joined the king in Payak. The king received Central Javanese reinforcements from Wanakĕrta, in Pajang (the district of Mataram proper was still in the power of his recalcitrant brother pangĕran Pugĕr).

p. 294. Captain Jonker did find Truna Jaya and the remainder of his followers (among whom were still some Makasarese gentlemen) in a retreat high up in the mountains. After some negotiation the Madurese prince unconditionally surrendered, forced by hunger to do so. His store of victuals was exhausted. He cast himself on the mercy of the V.O.C. commander.

p. 301. In Payak the Madurese prince met with a honourable treatment as a captive of the V.O.C. commander. But it always had been the king's wish to have him at his mercy. Mangku Rat was afraid of Truna Jaya's scheme to dissolve the alliance between the House of Mataram and the V.O.C., on which he depended to win his inheritance. Truna Jaya knew too much about Mangku Rat's dealings when he had been crownprince. The king therefore thought it best that he should die. During a ceremonial visit in the royal residence in Payak, Truna Jaya was personally stabbed with a criss by Mangku Rat and then finished off by his courtiers. Neither Jacob Couper, who was absent because of his illness, nor the V.O.C. government in Batavia gave much

credence to Mangku Rat's excuse for this deed, that Truna Jaya had
intended to murder him. Nevertheless the king was not called to account
for the death of the V.O.C. captive. It was thought that the country
was well rid of the troublesome Madurese prince. His followers were
also killed by the king's Central Javanese guardsmen.

———————

VII.

THE KAJORAN QUESTION
1680 - 1681

Summary of:

H. J. de Graaf, Het Kadjoran-vraagstuk. Jogjakarta 1940.
"Djåwå", *Tijdschrift van het Java-Instituut*. Vol. XX,
pp. 273-328.

VII. THE KAJORAN QUESTION

p. 273. The importance of Kajoran as a centre of opposition to Mataram rule in Central Java has previously not been recognized.

p. 274. According to Javanese historical tradition, the ancestor of the Kajoran family was a younger brother of ki gĕḍé Paṇḍan Arang, the holy man from Sĕmarang who introduced Islam to the southern districts of Central Java and was called sunan Tĕmbayat after the place were he was buried in the first half of the 16th century. The descendants of his younger brother, who was called sayyid Kalkum of Wot Galèh (a village situated near Tĕmbayat), settled in Kajoran not far away and became country gentlemen controlling extensive territories south of the present town of Klaṭèn. They were related by marriage to the Houses of Pajang (Pĕngging) and afterwards Mataram, especially to the Purbaya (Madyun) and Wira Mĕnggala branches of the latter.

p. 281. The great-grandson of the lord of Wot Galèh became known in Javanese history as Radèn Kajoran Ambalik (Radèn Kajoran the Deserter), because of his alliance with Truna Jaya, the Madurese prince whose insurrection nearly destroyed the House of Mataram. Truna Jaya was given a daughter of the Kajoran family as a wife. It was due to Radèn Kajoran's good offices that Truna Jaya, in accord with the crownprince of Mataram (later sunan Mangku Rat II), could establish himself as semi-independent ruler of Madura in the last years of the reign of Mangku Rat I.

p. 285. Truna Jaya took up residence in Surabaya in 1676. His Madurese captains took the most important towns of East Java and marched on Mataram. They reached the residence of Radèn Kajoran, on the eastern border of the district of Mataram, and were welcomed. Radèn Kajoran was disgusted with the misgovernment of the Mataram Court, and he nursed a grudge against Mangku Rat I for his cruelty in repressing popular religious movements. Further progress of the Madurese and Kajoran forces was stopped, however, by loyal Mataram troops commanded by the king's sons. Radèn Kajoran and his family and retainers retreated in good order under a Madurese escort to Surabaya to meet Truna Jaya. The borough of Kajoran was laid in ruin by the Mataram soldiery.

p. 289. Radèn Kajoran had an intimate knowledge of the state of the Mataram kingdom, and he was respected by religiously-minded circles in Central Java for his illustrious descent and his relation with the spiritual lords of Tĕmbayat. His advice was important to Truna Jaya in planning the campaign of 1677, which was a great success. Javanese auxiliaries from all districts of East Java reinforced Truna Jaya's Madurese troops, and they marched on Mataram in two columns, one from the east through Pajang and the other from the north through Kĕḍu. When the royal residence of Plèrèd was threatened by enemies, Mangku Rat and his sons left in a panic and retreated westward. The capital was plundered and burned, with the exception of the compounds of Truna Jaya's friends among the nobility, and the royal treasury was transported to Kaḍiri. After admiral Speelman's successful action against Surabaya, Truna Jaya had taken up his residence in the town of Kaḍiri, an old capital of the pre-Islamic kingdom of East Java.

p. 292. Truna Jaya did not aspire to become king of Mataram. As a descendant of the old pre-Islamic House of Majapahit, and as a Madurese prince, he felt at home only in East Java. There was some talk of a division of Java into an Eastern and a Western Kingdom, the latter to be ruled by the Kajoran family, but nothing came of it. Radèn Kajoran preferred for himself the position of a spiritual lord, and the family had no other suitable candidates for royalty.

p. 293. While in Kaḍiri Truna Jaya was attacked by his former ally (and son-in-law) the Makasarese kraèng of Galésong, whose loyalty was wavering. Truna Jaya saw fit to leave Kaḍiri for a short time, but in the end the kraèng was persuaded to retreat to his settlement in the Brantas delta and Truna Jaya returned. As far as was possible, Truna Jaya kept the noblemen who were on his side under his control in residences in the district of Kaḍiri. His uncle the pangéran of Sampang, called Cakra Ningrat II, was given a residence in Loḍaya in the south, and two Cĕrbon princes, sons of pangéran Giri Laya, were kept at Court until they escaped to Bantĕn during the brief Makasarese invasion of Kaḍiri. Radèn Kajoran resided in a resort at Totombo, in the hills south of Kaḍiri.

p. 294. He directed his emissaries, mostly itinerant traders, preachers and wandering students of religion, to travel throughout Java. It was known to the V.O.C. government that the Kajoran partisans in the interior of the country had connections with sympathizers among the religiously-minded citizens of the trading-towns on the North Coast. Therefore the Kajoran movement was considered to be a menace to the V.O.C., which aimed at a monopoly in the North Coast markets. Radèn

Kajoran's connection with religion and his popularity in trade circles increased in the course of time. Therefore princes like pangéran Pugěr, and the nobility in general, were reluctant to accept Radèn Kajoran's offers of cooperation in the struggle against Mangku Rat and his ally, the infidel V.O.C.

p. 298. Truna Jaya called his Madurese troops back from Mataram to Kaḍiri during his trouble with the kraèng of Galésong. Pangéran Pugěr's followers, mostly men from Bagelèn, the district west of Mataram, were unwilling to associate with the Kajoran partisans from the Pajang districts. Therefore the ruined capital of Plèrèd and the Mataram district (at the time afflicted by a terrible epidemic) were abondoned by Truna Jaya and Radèn Kajoran, and pangéran Pugěr established himself in the old centre of the kingdom. The Kajoran partisans retreated to their own district of Pajang. The territory of Těmbayat functioned as a buffer-state, so there was little fighting in the interior of Central Java for some time. Kajoran partisans and their Madurese allies were, however, active in the coastal districts east of Japara. Mangku Rat II, who had succeeded his father in the meantime, resided in Japara in the beginning of 1678. The few Javanese commanders who were loyal to him had a hard struggle to resist attacks by Kajoran partisans who had sympathizers among the citizens of the trading-towns.

p. 302. Radèn Kajoran left his temporary residence in Totombo and returned to his home in the hilly regions south of Pajang at the end of 1678, after Truna Jaya's capital in Kaḍiri was taken by the combined forces of the V.O.C. commander Antonio Hurdt and sunan Mangku Rat II. Radèn Kajoran took his way through the southern district of Panaraga, where he had many partisans, and established a new centre of religious and political action in Mlambang, in the Gunung Kidul district.

p. 303. He entered into an alliance with Raja Namrud (= Nimrod), a Makasarese adventurer who was a fugitive slave from Batavia and the leader of an ethnically-mixed group of Muslim fanatics. They had established a fortified position in the Banyumas district at Slinga (near Purbalingga) which they called Měsir (Egypt). Radèn Kajoran, who was not a fighter, began to be hard-pressed by Mangku Rat and his allies the V.O.C. companies of Bugis mercenaries, who returned to Central Java after their victory over Truna Jaya. Thus an alliance with the warlike Makasarese Raja seemed expedient. But Raja Namrud was forced by an action of the V.O.C. captain Jan Albert Sloot to abandon his plan to march on Mataram. The connection between the two religious leaders was broken. The Raja extended hospitality at Slinga to pangéran Pugĕr when the latter fled from Mataram, until he was pardoned and could return to Court. Raja Namrud held out in Slinga-Mĕsir till the end of 1681, when he was defeated in a campaign led by the V.O.C. commander Jacob Couper.

p. 307. Radèn Kajoran's last fortress in Mlambang was taken by a combined attack of Javanese forces led by Sindu Rĕja (who later became grandvizier) and European and Bugis V.O.C. companies under captain Sloot. The aged Javanese leader surrendered but was immediately executed upon the captain's order in September, 1678. His son-in-law Truna Jaya, who was not killed until January, 1680, survived him.

p. 308. The Kajoran movement, inspired by popular religious feelings, and supported by tradesfolk living in villages and boroughs in the country-side, did not immediately die after the fall of Mlambang. Three groups of partisans held out in the southern districts between Tĕmbayat and Kaḍuwang for several years: (1) close relatives of the Kajoran family, (2) men of religion from Tĕmbayat, and (3) men from Wanakusuma in the Gunung Kidul district.

p. 313. Mangku Rat II ordered a new royal residence to be built in Wanakĕrta, in the district of Pajang, and called it Kartasura. The old capital of Plèrèd, in Mataram, was ruined. The building activity began in 1680 but was soon interrupted by an attack of Kajoran partisans from the south, in alliance with local Pajang gentry who resented the occupation of their lands by the Mataram king. The attack was repulsed with some difficulty by the V.O.C. captain Sloot.

p. 314. Sloot also led a campaign against Tĕmbayat zealots, which ended in a massacre in the last months of 1680. The king was apprehensive of a popular religious uprising in the country-side and ordered the immediate execution of all men of religion who were made captive.

p. 315. Wanakusuma (now called Wanasari, in the district of Gunung Kidul) was the residence of the descendants of ki gĕḍé Giring, a contemporary of panĕmbahan Mataram and the head of an old native family, according to Javanese historical tradition. He was related by marriage to the Tĕmbayat family. Wanakusuma people marched on the newly built capital of Kartasura in 1681, but their attack was repulsed. A group of them continued their march northward and reached Dĕmak (the site of the holy mosque), but they were also defeated in the end.

p. 315. Some energetic Kajoran partisans established a connection with pangéran Pugĕr in the district of Bagĕlèn, and tried to persuade

him to persevere in his rebellion against his royal brother, but in vain.
The pangéran submitted and returned to Court in November, 1681.
The Kajoran people associated with Raja Namrud in Slinga, but their
time was past. The Raja's fortress was stormed and taken by the king's
troops soon afterwards.

p. 316. Meanwhile there was a new rising of Wanakusuma people
and a new attack on Kartasura, which was again repulsed by the V.O.C.
garrison in the fortress. In revenge, the village of Wanakusuma and
a holy cemetery there were destroyed by the king's Javanese forces in
the first months of 1682.

p. 317. Some Kajoran leaders escaped from Slinga after the defeat
of Raja Namrud and returned to Gunung Kidul, where they continued
their guerilla campaign against the king. They were arrested and
executed after some time.

p. 318. Wanakusuma people, allied with the rebellious Mataram
prince pangéran Silarong, and with a Kajoran kinsman, caused trouble
even in Tĕgal and Pĕkalongan, but they were also killed. The last great
effort by Wanakusuma men to drive away the Mataram king failed
in 1683. The king's forces commanded by pangéran Pugĕr (who wanted
to show his loyalty) gained some victories and there was again a massacre. The last scions of the House of Wanakusuma-Giring joined the
Balinese adventurer Surapati, whose star was just rising at the time.

p. 320. Kajoran, Wanakusuma, Tĕmbayat and Giri were important
spiritual centres and the residences of ancient religious families whose
authority in the country-side equalled, and sometimes even eclipsed, the
king's. There are several more religious leaders mentioned in Javanese
books on history and in Dutch reports, including the journal of Antonio
Hurdt's campaign (see the present summary, V). A remarkable in-
stance of defiance of royalty by a popular man of religion was the
attack of an "ajar" called Téja Laku of mount Kĕlud with 40 followers
armed with chopping-knives, on the camp of Mangku Rat II during
the siege of Kaḍiri in 1678. The 40 zealots ran amuck and were killed
by the grandvizier's Javanese guardsmen. Téja Laku is reported by
Javanese tradition to have been invulnerable; he could only be slain
by the king himself, handling a holy lance. There was, of course, a
difference in social standing between the spiritual lords of Giri and
Tĕmbayat who were the heads of ancient families, and popular holy
men from mountain recesses. The kings of the House of Mataram never
felt entirely safe as long as the authority of men of religion, whatever
their standing, was recognized in the country.

p. 322. The political failure of the Kajoran movement in Central Java and the return of Mangku Rat II to the throne of the kingdom were due to several factors. One of them was the incapacity of the Kajoran, Tĕmbayat and Wanakusuma partisans to produce a suitable candidate for kingship. Their leaders were men of religion, countrymen and tradesfolk who were insufficiently interested in ruling the country.

p. 324. Appendices: a list of Javanese and Dutch books on the history of the period; a chronological list of events from 1624 (annexation of Madura by Sultan Agung of Mataram) to 1685 (the last Wanakusuma partisans join Surapati); genealogical trees of the Kajoran and Tĕmbayat family (mentioning Giring and Wanakusuma, and ending with Nĕrang Kusuma, grandvizier of Kartasura from 1680-1686 under Mangku Rat II); and an old Dutch translation of a Javanese letter sent by Radèn Kajoran to adipati Martapura of Paṭi to persuade him to side with the Kajoran party.

VIII.

THE MURDER OF CAPTAIN FRANÇOIS TACK
FEBRUARY 1686

Summary of:

H. J. de Graaf, De moord op Kapitein François Tack,
8 Febr. 1686. Amsterdam 1935. Proefschrift Leiden.
(Ph.D. Thesis Leiden University 1935).

VIII. CAPTAIN TACK'S DEATH

Chpt. 1, *p. 1.* *General introduction on Javanese dynastic history*

Chpt. 2. *Notes on Dutch and Javanese sources*

p. 4. The history of Surapati, the Balinese condottiere who killed captain Tack, is not well known.*

Chpt. 3. *The state of the Mataram kingdom during the first years of the reign of sunan Mangku Rat II, 1677-'82*

p. 9. The king's enemies were: (1) the insurgent Madurese prince Truna Jaya, (2) his ally the Makasarese kraèng of Galésong, (3) the aged spiritual lord of Giri, (4) Radèn Kajoran, and (5) Raja Namrud. All these were defeated successively in campaigns led by V.O.C. captains. Mangku Rat II was escorted to the old royal residence of Plèrèd by the V.O.C. commander Jacob Couper in November, 1680. The old Mataram capital appeared to be in ruins, and the king therefore made the momentous decision to leave the remote inland district of Mataram and to build a new capital in the district of Pajang. The new Court of Kartasura was more accessible for V.O.C. envoys and troops coming from Sĕmarang, and had better connections with East Java. A fortress with a V.O.C. garrison was established opposite the royal residence as a permanent guard against invaders. Pangéran Pugĕr, who had defied his royal brother's authority after 1677 and had also called himself susuhunan, finally submitted and was pardoned in 1681. In Kartasura, in the district where the Sultan of Pajang had reigned a century before, Javanese trade and industry (such as batik dyeing) began to develop in cooperation with Chinese and other foreign traders and artisans. Javanese literature and art found patrons at Court. The king and some influential courtiers had travelled widely over Central and East Java for several years and had acquired more culture than their predecessors had possessed.

---

* Some Javanese legendary tales on Surapati's exploits have been discussed by Mrs Ann Kumar in: "Surapati, Portrait of a Hero in Javanese Literature" (Thesis Canberra University, Australia, 1969).

p. 14. The kyahi of Wanakusuma, a kinsman of the great Radèn
Kajoran, and his followers in the hilly region along the South Coast
were troublesome during the first years of the reign. They were inspired
by popular Islamic belief in prophecies and miracles. An action by the
V.O.C. garrison of Kartasura prevented a group of Islamic zealots from
Bantĕn from joining the Wanakusuma partisans. The last of them were
defeated and massacred by the king's troops in October, 1683.

p. 18. An anti-V.O.C. faction began to develop at the Kartasura
Court from 1681. Its head was the new patih (grandvizier) Nĕrang
Kusuma, who was related to the Kajoran, Tĕmbayat and Wanakusuma
families. Ladies at Court promoted his rise in the king's favour. Mangku
Rat's religious feelings and his family pride were played upon in order
to estrange his from the V.O.C.

p. 21. The points on which the king was particularly sensitive were
(1) the payment of the debt incurred to the V.O.C. since 1677, (2) the
cession of territories to the V.O.C., (3) the mercantile privileges and
freedom from duties accorded to V.O.C. trade, (4) the unseemly
behaviour of some V.O.C. officers in the trading-posts on the North
Coast, and (5) the permanent presence of the V.O.C. garrison in
Kartasura, which he found annoying. The cession of sovereign rights
in Sĕmarang, Japara and Rĕmbang, which was stipulated in the contracts, was ignored as far as possible by local Javanese officials. Makasarese and Balinese adventurers and soldiers of fortune were welcomed
in Kartasura by the anti-V.O.C. faction.

Chpt. 4.   *Prelude to the outbreak of hostilities in Kartasura*

p. 32. Johannes Cops, a new factor of the V.O.C. trading-post in
Sĕmarang, was sent as an envoy to investigate the situation at the
Kartasura Court in September, 1684. In return, important Javanese
courtiers travelled to Batavia to compliment the new governor-general
Johannes Camphuys on his election in the beginning of 1685. They
brought a letter containing a memorial of the king's grievances, but
the Javanese envoys were sent home without a satisfactory reply.

p. 37. In the meantime Surapati's star was rising at the Kartasura
Court. He was of Balinese origin, probably born in the Eastern Corner
of Java about 1660. He escaped from slavery in Batavia and collected
a band of outlaws of various descent in the mountainous districts of
West Java. The band enlisted as a volunteer corps with the V.O.C.
forces stationed in the Priangan highlands, but Untung (Surapati's
name in Batavia) quarreled with a Dutch officer, killed a number of

V.O.C. soldiers, and made his escape eastward. The V.O.C. commander
Jacob Couper failed to find him in the highlands during an expedition
started from Cĕrbon, and Surapati became the most ferocious and
dreaded of outlaws, living from blackmail and robbery in the hilly districts
of Banyumas and Bagĕlèn. The local Javanese authorities could not
overcome him. The cunning grand-vizier of Kartasura Nĕrang Kusuma
saw fit to use Surapati to master other unruly elements in Banyumas
and Bagĕlèn. The headman of outlaws was made a condottiere of a
volunteer corps in the king's service. He was called to Court, pardoned
and given a residence near the capital of Kartasura, where he reinforced
the anti-V.O.C. faction. The king was caught between his anti-V.O.C.
courtiers and military men and the V.O.C., his ally to whom he was
indebted for all he had. He tried to compromise in letters sent to Batavia,
and he paid instalments of his debt. The V.O.C. government decided
to help him by sending captain François Tack, the victor over Truna
Jaya and a person well-known to the king, as plenipotentiary to Kartasura in November, 1685. Tack was ordered to arrest Surapati, if need
be by force. Aside from this, his mission was one of appeasement.

   p. 48.   In the eastern part of the kingdom, confusion had arisen
after the king's departure for Mataram in November, 1680. Madura
had been divided between Truna Jaya's uncle Cakra Ningrat (II), who
had been pardoned, in the west, and Yuda Nagara, Truna Jaya's old
governor who could not be dislodged, in the east. After Yuda Nagara's
death in Sumĕnĕp in 1684, Cakra Ningrat tried to expand his influence
over the whole of the island, and also in East Java. A Madurese pirate
and former captain of Truna Jaya called Wasèng Rana served him.
Jang Rana, the king's governor of Surabaya, was his son-in-law. Jang
Rana, formerly called Angga Wangsa, and his brother Angga Jaya,
the governor of Pasuruhan, were of Balinese descent. The rulers of the
district of Blambangan in the Eastern Corner of Java were members
of the Tawang Alun family who had defied the authority of the
Mataram kings since 1670. Blambangan bands were even seen marauding in the district of Kaḍiri. The V.O.C. sent Jeremias van Vliet
with a small expeditionary force to Surabaya in March, 1685. The
pirate Wasèng Rana was arrested and executed, and a temporary
arrangement of the succession in East Madura was agreed upon. In
a conference with the king's governors of East Java and Madura from
Tuban to Sumĕnĕp, convened in Surabaya in July, 1685, van Vliet
made them promise to keep the peace and to fight the Blambangan
and Balinese invaders in a concerted action. But nothing came of this.

There were no V.O.C. forces available to launch an offensive in remote districts.

Chpt. 5. *Captain Tack's progress from Batavia to Kartasura, late 1685*

p. 58. Captain Tack touched at the port of Cĕrbon to inspect the trading-post. He persuaded Sultan Anom, the most active of the three Cĕrbon rulers, to accompany him to Kartasura in order to deliberate with the king and the East Javanese governors on the state of Java. During his stay in Japara, captain Tack saw the advisability of moving the centre of V.O.C. activity in the Javanese kingdom to Sĕmarang, which had easier access for envoys coming from the interior of the country. The Batavia government followed his advice some years later.

p. 61. The situation of the royal residence and the V.O.C. fortress in Kartasura is fairly well known from a Dutch map made shortly after the fateful events. The V.O.C. fortress contained only some bamboo buildings and sheds. The officer in command, lieutenant Greving, was a good soldier but not a perspicacious diplomat. The military stores were insufficient.

p. 65. Captain Tack had to wait in Sĕmarang for an escort of important courtiers which was to lead him in state to Kartasura. During the month of preparations before the plenipotentiary's arrival, both the king and the anti-V.O.C. faction at Court became nervous. The anti-V.O.C. faction, which had the sympathy and even the secret support of the grand-vizier Nĕrang Kusuma, sent letters, seemingly in the king's name, to a headman of Malay pirates on the coast of the island of Blitung (Billiton) who was supposed to be a servant of the Sultan of Mĕnangkabau (in the interior of Sumatra), to ask for assistance in the imminent war with the infidel V.O.C. The letters were intercepted by a vigilant V.O.C. officer in Tĕgal and sent to Batavia. Islamic religious agitation was noticed in various parts of the Archipelago at the time.

p. 73. Surapati, Cakra Ningrat of Madura, whose loyalties were doubtful, the grand-vizier Nĕrang Kusuma, lieutenant Greving and the king had many deliberations in the capital. Hoping to make a favourable impression on captain Tack, who was about to arrive, Cakra Ningrat organized an attack of Madurese and Javanese guardsmen on Surapati's Balinese settlement near the royal residence of Kartasura, in order to force him to surrender his arms. The attack was repulsed; probably it had not been meant seriously. The grand-vizier seems to have encouraged Surapati in his confidence that he could defy the V.O.C. with impunity. He proved to be right in the end.

Chpt. 6.   *The death of captain Tack and his men,*
   8th of February, 1686

p. 84. The plenipotentiary, his companies of V.O.C. soldiers and his Javanese escort arrived in Kartasura just after the faked attack on Surapati's settlement. Captain Tack took over command of all V.O.C. forces, put strong guards before the royal residence and the fortress for safety, and marched out himself with a small force to look for Surapati, who was reported to be retreating eastward. But the crafty Balinese fighter turned back with a small band, unseen by Tack, and attacked the V.O.C. guard before the royal residence. He killed lieutenant Greving and his men and set the guardhouse on fire. Captain Tack was alarmed and returned immediately. Surapati and his fighters were caught between the buildings of the royal residence behind them where the fire was spreading even in the private mosque, and the V.O.C. companies armed with muskets in front of them on the *alun-alun* (great square in front of the royal compound). After several sallies which were repulsed, the Balinese ran amuck and succeeded in reaching the ranks of the soldiers before the muskets could be reloaded. In the following hand-to-hand fight (bayonets not yet being in use), most of the Dutch officers and men, including captain Tack, were killed by lance-thrusts. One lieutenant and the rest of the soldiers, partly disarmed and wounded, made their escape to the fortress which was nearby. It was believed that Balinese volunteers in the king's service, and even some Javanese in Balinese clothes, had taken part in the final amuck-running. The end of the day was celebrated as a victory by the playing of gamĕlans inside the royal compound. The dead and wounded Dutch military men were brought into the fortress without molestation in the course of the afternoon.

Chpt. 7.   *The retreat of the V.O.C. garrison from Kartasura*
   to Sĕmarang

p. 101. Surapati and his Balinese followers left Kartasura the same afternoon. They had suffered heavy losses. Surapati continued his march eastward in the direction of his native country. He had never seriously intended to settle in Mataram. Captain Leeman, the commander of the V.O.C. fortress in Kartasura, was not attacked. He succeeded in restoring order in the weakened garrison, kept control of the V.O.C.

allies from Cĕrbon (Sultan Anom and his retinue) and Sumĕnĕp (the provisionally-appointed governor), maintained outwardly friendly relations with the king, and corresponded with headquarters in Japara by means of express messengers. This journey took three days at the least. The king was extremely nervous and afraid of retaliations. Repeatedly protesting his innocence and expressing his regret, he declared that he had ordered his troops to pursue Surapati and to hunt him down, but nothing came of it. The anti-V.O.C. faction at Court sabotaged all such action. The king's fear of V.O.C. retaliation was counterbalanced by his knowledge that Surapati had friends in Kartasura. Perhaps even Mangku Rat himself secretly admired the Balinese adventurer's boldness.

p. 107. On learning what had happened in Kartasura, the V.O.C. government in Batavia decided that the garrison should retreat to Sĕmarang. Both the risk of leaving the garrison in Kartasura, and the expenses of sending reinforcements were deemed too great. Captain Leeman succeeded in gently familiarizing the king with the idea that the V.O.C. garrison and even his Dutch bodyguard, which he had had at his disposal for years, would leave. Mangku Rat was told that all the V.O.C. forces were needed in East Java to fight Surapati, which was partly true. The captain brought his troops and the V.O.C. possessions in the Kartasura fortress safely to Sĕmarang under difficult circumstances, arriving there at the end of March, 1686. The fortress of Kartasura was abandoned.

Chpt. 8. *Repercussions of the Surapati troubles in the Pasisir districts and measures taken by the V.O.C. government*

p. 111. The V.O.C. fortress on the Dana Raja hill commanding Japara was immediately put into a state of defence. By a lucky chance, V.O.C. troop ships destined for the Spice Islands arrived in Japara just in time. Their appearance overawed those V.O.C. allies and auxiliaries whose allegiance was wavering. Smaller V.O.C. trading-posts such as Dĕmak, Grĕsik and Rĕmbang were closed and some were even abandoned. Many letters and envoys were exchanged between Kartasura, Japara and Batavia. The king dismissed Nĕrang Kusuma from his service (but without punishing him), and appointed Sindu Rĕja, a military man, in his place as grand-vizier. Mangku Rat expressed his willingness to travel personally to Japara (which he knew well) and even to Batavia to explain matters. There were also rumours of a royal pilgrimage to the holy mosque of Dĕmak. But since no forceful action or retaliation by the V.O.C. government was forthcoming, the king regained self-confidence. The inactivity of the V.O.C. troops in Japara and the undisturbed development of Surapati's dominion in East Java made it possible for the anti-V.O.C. faction at Court to reassert itself.

p. 127. Javanese and Chinese officials in Sěmarang who cooperated with the V.O.C. in the trading-post suffered vexations from the Kartasura Court. After a considerable delay the king sent well-qualified envoys to Batavia at the end of 1686, but the contents of the letters which they brought was found unsatisfactory. The V.O.C. government took the view that the Central Javanese kingdom should be left alone for the time being. Relations between Kartasura and Batavia were not openly hostile, but at the best were stiffly formal during the rest of the reign of Mangku Rat II, who died in 1703.

p. 131. Surapati and his Balinese fighters, continuing their march eastward after the Kartasura incident, were pursued by the king's Javanese troops without any alacrity. They were allowed to escape several times. Surapati succeeded in reaching the Eastern Corner of Java, his native area, by way of Kaḍiri and Bangil. The Mataram king's governors of Pasuruhan, Bangil and Prabalingga either left their posts or went over to the side of Surapati, who established a Court in Pasuruhan and called himself henceforth Wira Nagara. He acquired control of all Eastern Corner districts east of Surabaya as far as Blambangan. Adventurers from many other areas of South East Asia and India were attracted by his good fortune and joined his banners. His rule was not seriously imperilled by attacks of Cakra Ningrat's bands. Madura and Surabaya were not inclined to fight for the integrity of the Mataram kingdom, which had destroyed their own independence less than a century before.

Chpt. 9. *The last years of the reign of Mangku Rat II, 1687-1703*

p. 135. Relations between the Kartasura Court and Pasuruhan were ambiguous. If there was some fighting, it was mostly sham. The king wanted to uphold his authority in the eyes of his subjects in Central and West Java and in those of the V.O.C. government in Batavia. Therefore he made a show of severity in his dealings with Surapati. The V.O.C. government was deceived by this at first. But after some time V.O.C. officers in Surabaya began to see through the trick of sham fighting and reported it to Batavia. No action was taken, however.

p. 139. Mangku Rat's suzerainty was formally acknowledged by Surapati in 1687. In that year he paid an official visit to Court, in the company of East Javanese local rulers who had taken his side and envoys from a Balinese king, as well as a strong bodyguard. Attempts to murder him unawares in Kartasura were frustrated by his vigilance, and he never again visited the Court. Nevertheless this visit was a success for the Kartasura Court's diplomacy. The dismissed grand-vizier Něrang Kusuma, who was known for his anti-V.O.C. feelings, was employed as the king's representative at the Pasuruhan Court to the end of Mangku Rat's reign.

p. 142. Meanwhile the Kartasura Court succeeded also in maintaining stiffly formal relations with the V.O.C. officials in Japara and Batavia. The debt incurred in the beginning of the reign was paid off by fairly regular annual instalments, so that the outstanding amount dwindled down perceptibly. The economy of the Javanese kingdom adapted itself to altered circumstances. Crops in demand for overseas trade were cultivated, money circulation increased, and Chinese traders made their appearance in the interior of the country.

p. 145. Mangku Rat II, like his father before him, became ill and lost interest in state affairs as he grew older. The crownprince (later Mangku Rat III, called Mangku Rat Mas) was an only son, and rather unruly. His entourage nursed anti-V.O.C. feelings. The Kartasura Court was at times full of rumours about heroic actions to be taken against the infidel foreigners, but nothing came of it.

p. 146. Cakra Ningrat, sent by the king to East Java to arrest Surapati in 1686, understood well enough that for his dominions in West Madura peace and order in the Pasisir harbours was of more importance than the integrity of the inland Mataram kingdom. Therefore his fighting against Surapati was only sham. The men of West Madura had fought on the side of Truna Jaya a few years before, and Truna Jaya and Surapati seemed to have much in common. Batavia's hope that Cakra Ningrat would overcome Surapati proved idle. The Madurese prince had also to consider anti-V.O.C. and Islamic religious feelings in his own surroundings.

p. 147. Pangéran Pugěr, who had been pardoned in 1681, was still considered to be a likely successor of his brother Mangku Rat II. He commanded a large following in Mataram, having ruled there as a king from 1677 to 1681. He was distrusted by the crownprince's party, who were anti-V.O.C. So pangéran Pugěr entered into a private and secret correspondence with V.O.C. authorities with a view to the possibility that he might succeed his brother. In fact he did become king, under the name of Paku Buwana I, instead of the crownprince, after having ceded large territories and renounced important rights in favour of the V.O.C.

p. 148. Surapati's rule in the Eastern Corner of Java remained practically unchallenged until 1691. In that year the aged king of Blambangan, Tawang Alun, died. Troughout his life he had maintained an independent position between the Balinese kingdom in the east and the rulers of East Java, who were Mataram subjects, in the west. One of his sons feared Surapati's aggressiveness and approached the V.O.C. in Batavia for help. This was considered to be an opportunity to begin an attack on Surapati from the east by supporting the Blambangan forces. But then in 1697 a successful invasion of Balinese troops from Badung (Dèn Pasar), supported by Surapati, overthrew the native dynasty and put an end to Blambangan's independence.

p. 153. In connection with these events in the Eastern Corner of Java, the V.O.C. decided to move its headquarters in Central Java from Japara to Sĕmarang, where a strong and modern fortress was to be built. This had already been advised by admiral Speelman and captain Tack. The preparations for the fortress in Sĕmarang brought about a new outburst of anti-V.O.C. sentiment at the Kartasura Court. There were rumours of a planned surprise attack on Japara of Balinese fighting men in disguise, but it was not executed. In 1693, Chinese rioters attacked the V.O.C. trading-post in Japara but were repulsed with some difficulty. When brought to trial, they accused the Kartasura Court of complicity. The Chinese traders residing in the king's states were legally V.O.C. subjects according to the contracts. They had been put under locally-appointed Chinese officers, who were subordinate to the shahbandar of Japara (afterwards of Sĕmarang). But the increasing number of Chinese immigrants, who were attracted by the development of economy and trade in Java since the establishment of the V.O.C. in Batavia, could not be controlled by a few local officers. There was friction between factions of Chinese traders. (An explosion of Chinese rioting later led to the destruction of the royal residence of Kartasura in 1742).

p. 158. Relations between Mangku Rat II and the V.O.C. government finally grew rather more friendly in 1694, when an envoy from Japara, the first one since captain Tack's death in 1686, appeared in Kartasura. But by then the king's authority in his own capital was dwindling and the crownprince's faction had won the upper hand at Court. Bands of Surapati's Balinese and East Javanese followers were seen marauding not far from Kartasura. Mangku Rat felt unsafe, and the grand-vizier Sindu Rĕja travelled to Semarang on his own authority to deliberate with V.O.C. authorities on the state of the Javanese kingdom.

p. 164. Mangku Rat II died in his dotage in November, 1703. The crownprince had made sure of the support of important courtiers beforehand, and ascended the throne as Mangku Rat III. There is a story that he tried to keep his uncle pangéran Pugĕr in seclusion, practically as a captive, in Kartasura, but the pangéran's numerous followers helped him to escape to Sĕmarang in 1704. Having come to an agreement with the V.O.C. authorities, Pugĕr was acknowledged by them as the rightful king, and was escorted back to Kartasura by V.O.C. troops in 1705, there to reign as susuhunan Paku Buwana I (1703-'19). This was, for the time being, the end of the anti-V.O.C. faction at Court. Mangku Rat III took refuge with Surapati in East Java. After Surapati's death in 1706, he surrendered in Malang to the V.O.C. commander Govert Knol in 1708. The V.O.C. government decided to send him with his family and retinue to exile in Ceylon, an expedient used to eliminate troublesome princes on several occasions afterwards. He died in Ceylon in 1737. His family was then allowed to return to Java.

Chpt. 10. *Conclusion*

p. 167. Captain Tack was sent to Kartasura in 1686 with a mission of appeasement, but this was imperfectly understood at Court. His violent death marked the beginning of a period which was to end in political and armed interventions by the V.O.C. in the affairs of the Javanese kingdom of a more drastic and sweeping character than had originally been the intention in Batavia, and certainly in Amsterdam. The "murder" of captain François Tack was a turning-point in Javanese dynastic history.

Appendices

I. Old Dutch caption belonging to an illustration in Nic. de Graaff's "Reisen . . . naar alle gewesten des Werelds", 1939-1687 (Linschoten-Vereeniging, vol. 33, p. 197 and 198).

II. Old Dutch translations of Javanese letters which make it probable that the attack on captain Tack was premeditated by the anti-V.O.C. faction at Court.

––––––––

KEY

to the Roman serial numbers used in the Comprehensive List of Sources and the General Index of Names to indicate Dr de Graaf's eight books and articles on Javanese history, and the Summary.

I Graaf, H. J. de, en Pigeaud, Th. G. Th. De eerste Moslimse Vor-stendommen op Java. Studiën over de staatkundige Geschiedenis van de 15e en 16e eeuw. 's-Gravenhage, 1974.

> Verhandelingen v.h. Kon. Instituut voor Taal-, Land- en Volkenkunde, vol. 69.

II Graaf, H. J. de. De Regering van panembahan Sénapati Inga-laga. 's-Gravenhage, 1954.

> Verhandelingen v.h. Kon. Instituut voor Taal-, Land- en Volkenkunde, vol. 13.

III Graaf, H. J. de. De Regering van sultan Agung, vorst van Mataram, 1613-1645, en die van zijn voorganger panembahan Séda-ing-Krapjak, 1601-1613. 's-Gravenhage, 1958.

> Verhandelingen v.h. Kon. Instituut voor Taal-, Land- en Volkenkunde, vol. 23.

IV-1, IV-2 Graaf, H. J. de. De Regering van sunan Mangku Rat I Tĕgal Wangi, vorst van Mataram, 1646-1677. 2 vols. 's-Graven-hage, 1961-1962. I. De Ontbinding van het Rijk. II. Opstand en Ondergang.

> Verhandelingen v.h. Kon. Instituut voor Taal-, Land- en Volkenkunde, vols. 33 and 39.

V Graaf, H. J. de (ed.). De Expeditie van Anthonio Hurdt, Raad van Indië, als Admiraal en Superintendent naar de Binnenlanden van Java, sept.-dec. 1678, volgens het Journaal van Johan Jurgen Briel, secretaris. Met een inleiding en aantekeningen van —. 's-Gravenhage, 1971.

> Werken uitgegeven door de Linschoten-Vereeniging, vol. LXXII.

VI Graaf, H. J. de. Gevangenneming en Dood van Raden Truna-Djaja, from

> "Tijdschrift voor Ind. Taal-, Land- en Volkenkunde", Batavia-Jakarta, vol. LXXXV, 1952, pp. 273-309.

VII Graaf, H. J. de. Het Kadjoran-vraagstuk, from
"Djawa", Jogjakarta, vol. XX, 1940, pp. 273-328.

VIII Graaf, H. J. de. De Moord op Kapitein François Tack, 8 febr.
1686. Amsterdam, 1935.
   Ph.D. Thesis, University of Leiden.

IX Pigeaud, Theodore G. Th., and Graaf, H. J. de. Islamic States
in Java, 1500-1700. Eight Dutch books and articles by Dr H. J.
de Graaf as summarized by Theodore G. Th. Pigeaud, with a
Comprehensive List of Sources and a General Index of Names
composed by H. J. de Graaf. The Hague, 1976.
   Verhandelingen v.h. Kon. Instituut voor Taal-, Land- en Volkenkunde,
vol. 70.

BIBLIOGRAPHY

COMPREHENSIVE LIST OF SOURCES

for the study of Javanese history, 1500-1700, mentioned in Dr de Graaf's eight books and articles. The Roman serial numbers in italics, *I-VIII*, at the end of the titles refer to the book(s) or article(s) where the indicated source material was used.

ABBREVIATIONS USED IN THE BIBLIOGRAPHICAL LIST

K.B.G.	Koninklijk Bataviaasch Genootschap voor Kunsten en Wetenschappen.
K.I.	Koninklijk Instituut voor Taal-, Land- en Volkenkunde.
Verh.	Verhandelingen.
T.B.G.	Tijdschrift van het Kon. Bataviaasch Genootschap.
B.K.I.	Bijdragen van het Kon. Instituut voor T., L. en Vk.
B.P.	Balai Poestaka (Volkslectuur).
L.U.B.	Leidse Universiteitsbibliotheek.
L.V.	Linschoten-Vereeniging (Dutch "Hakluyt Society").
gesch.	geschiedenis, history.
hist.	historical
proefschr.	proefschrift (dissertation, doctor's thesis).

Adam, L. Eenige historische en legendarische plaatsnamen in Jogjakarta. "Djawa" X 1930, p. 150. *III, IV.*

— Geschiedkundige aanteekeningen omtrent de residentie Madioen. "Djawa" XVIII-XIX 1938-1939. *I, V.*

Admonitions (The) of Seh Bari. A 16th century Jav. Muslim text attributed to the saint of Bonang, re-edited and transl. with an introduction by G. W. J. Drewes. The Hague 1969. Uitg. K.I. Bibl. Indonesica 4. *I.*

Akkeren, P. v., Shri and Christ. A study of the indigenous Church in East Java. London (1970). *I.*

Archief (Koloniaal), Archives, in het Algemeen Rijksarchief te 's-Gravenhage, waarin Generale Missiven (tot 1697 uitgeg. door W. Ph. Coolhaas in Rijks Geschiedkundige Publicatiën). *II-V.*
Resolutiën der Hooge Regeering te Batavia. *V.*
Inkomend Bataviaasch Briefboek. *III-V.*

Atja. Tjarita purwaka Tjaruban (Sedjarah Muladjadi Tjirebon). Djakarta 1972. Seri monografi Museum no. 5. *I.*

Babad Bla-Batuh, uitgeg. door C. C. Berg. De geschiedenis van een tak der familie Jelantik. Santpoort 1932. Uitgaven v.d. Kirtya Liefrinck-v. d. Tuuk te Singaradja. Jav.-Balische Hist. Geschriften no. II. *I*.

Babad Bulèlèng. A Balinese dynastic Genealogy by P. J. Worsley. The Hague 1972. Bibl. Indonesica 8. *I*.

Babad Grĕsik, hs. L.U.B. cod. Or. 6780. *I*.

Babad Mataram. Serat Babad ing Mataram djil. I, ingkang ngedalaken rd. Dirdja Satmadja. Alb. Rusche & Co. Soerakarta 1904. *V*.

Babad Pasaréan ing Grĕsik, hs. L.U.B. cod Or. 858a. *I*.

Babad Sangkala. Copy of ms. Bijbelgenootschap 87 (XIII). Ms. K.B.G. 608, coll. Brandes. *I-IV*.

Babad Tanah Djawi. Batavia-C. 1939-1941. 24 dln. uitg. Balé Pustaka serie no. 1289. *I-V*.

Babad Tanah Djawi, in proza. Jav. gesch. loopende tot het jaar 1647 der Jav. jaartelling, uitgeg. door J. J. Meinsma. 2e dr. 's-Gravenhage 1884, 1899. 2 stukken (Jav. tekst) uitg. K.I. *I-VIII*.

— naar de uitg. van J. J. Meinsma, vertaald door W. L. Olthof, 's-Gravenhage (1941). 2 dln. (Met) Register ... samengesteld door A. Teeuw. *I-VIII*.

Babad Tanah Djawi no. 3 Serat Babad ing Tanah Djawi, angka 3. Van Dorp, Semarang-Surabaya 1912. *V*.

Babad Tjerbon. Uitvoerige inhoudsopgave en noten door ... J. L. A. Brandes, met inleid. en bijbehoorende tekst uitgeg. door D. A. Rinkes. Bat.-'s-Hage 1911. Verh. K.B.G. LIX ii 1e ged. *I-III*.

Babad Tuban, ed. Tan Khoen Swie, Kadiri, 3de dr. 1936. *I, III, IV*.

Bangsacara en Ragapadmi, een verhaal van Madoera, vertaald door Dr Th. Pigeaud. Djawa XII 1932, p. 186. *I*.

Barros, J. de. Da Asia ... Nova Edição ... Lisboa 1777-78. 5 tomos en 9 partes. *I-III*.

Begin ende Voortgangh van de Ver. Geoctroyeerde O.I. Compagnie. Vervattende de voornaemste Reysen ... Amsterdam 1646. 2 dln. I Veerthien Voyagien II ... twaalf Voyagien. *II, III*.

Berg, C. C. Bijdragen tot de kennis der Panji-verhalen. B.K.I. CX 1954, p. 305-334. *I*.

— De Middeljav. historische Traditie. Santpoort 1927. Proefschr. *I-III*.

— see Kidung Pamancangah and Pranatjitra.

Berg, L. W. C. v. d. De Mohammedaansche Geestelijkheid en de geestelijke Goederen op Java en Madoera. T.B.G. XXVII 1882, p. 44. *I*.

Bogaert, A. Historische Reizen door de Oostersche deelen van Asia ... Amsterdam 1711. *I*.

Bosch, F. D. K. Het Lingga-heiligdom van Dinaja. T.B.G. LXV 1924, p. 227. *I, II*.

Bouwstoffen voor de geschiedenis der Nederlanders in den Maleischen Archipel. Uitgeg. en toegel. door P. A. Tiele en J. E. Heeres, 's-Grav. 1886-1895. 3 dln. *III.*

Bouwstoffen voor de geschiedenis der Prot. Kerk in Ned.-Indië. Bijeengebr. door J. Mooij. 2e en 3e dl. Welt. 1929, 1931. *IV, V.*

Brandes, J. Arya Penangsang's rechten en pogingen tot herstel daarvan. T.B.G. XLIII 1900, p. 88. *I, II.*

— Djakuwès in de Babad, tijdens de Belegering van Batavia, Jacques Lefebre. T.B.G. XLIV 1901, p. 286. *III.*

— Register op de proza-omzetting van de Babad Tanah Djawi. Verh. K.B.G. 1900. *I.*

— Yogyakarta. T.B.G. XXXVII 1894, p. 41. *III.*

Brascamp, L. H. B. Houtleveranties onder de O.I. Compagnie. T.B.G. LIX-LXI 1919-1922 (passim). *IV.*

Bröndsted, Joh. Vore gamle Tropenkolonier. Kopenhagen 1952-53 2 dln. *IV.*

Bruin, Corn. de. Reizen over Moskovië door Perzië en Indië . . . Amsteldam 1714. *I, II.*

Brumund, J. F. G. Bijdragen tot de kennis van het Hindoeïsme op Java. Verh. (K.)B.G. XXXIII 1860. *I.*

— Indiana. Verzameling van stukken van onderscheiden aard, over . . . den Indischen Archipel . . . uitgeg. door H. A. G. Brumund. Amsterdam 1853-1854. 2 dln. in 1 band. *I.*

Calendar of State Papers, Colonial Series II, IV, VI, VIII. East Indies... 1617-1634. Edited by W. N. Sainsbury. London 1870-1892. 4 vols. *III, IV, VI, VIII.*

Calendar of the Court Minutes of the East India Company, 1674-76. Vol. IX. Ed. Ethel Bruce Sainsbury and W. Foster. Oxford 1935. *IV.*

Castanheda, Fernão Lopez de. Historia dos Descobrimentos y Conquistas da India pelos Portugueses. Nova ed. livro I-VIII. Lisboa 1833. 7 vols. *I.*

Cense, A. A. Enige aantekeningen over Makassaars-Boeginese geschiedschrijving. B.K.I. CVII 1951, p. 42. *III.*

— De Kroniek van Bandjarmasin. Santpoort 1928. Proefschr. *I-IV.*

— De Verering van sjeich Jusuf in Zuid-Celebes. Bingkisan Budi, 1950, p. 50. *IV.*

Clercq, F. S. A. Eene episode uit de gesch. van Madjapahit. T.B.G. XXIV 1877, p. 280. *I.*

Coen, Jan Pietersz. Bescheiden omtrent zijn bedrijf in Indië. Dl. 1-5, verzameld door H. T. Colenbrander, 's-Grav. 1919-1923. Uitg. K.I. *I-III.*

Coen, Jan Pietersz. Bescheiden enz. dl. 7-8, verzameld door W. Ph. Coolhaas. 's-Grav. 1952-1953. Uitg. K.I. *I-III.*

— Vertoogh van den Staat der Ver. Nederlanden in ... O. Indiën. Kroniek Hist. Genootschap te Utrecht. Utr. 1855, p. 126. *II.*

Cohen Stuart, A. B. Over de beschreven balken ... uit de troonzaal van ... Martapoera in Bandjarmasin. T.B.G. XVII 1869, p. 548. *I.*

Colenbrander, H. T. Levensbeschrijving van J. Pz. Coen. 6e dl. van Jan Pz. Coen. Bescheiden enz. 's-Grav. 1924. Uitg. K.I. *III.*

Cornets de Groot Sr., A. D. Statistiek van Java. Residentie Grissee 1822. Ms. K.I. no. H 379. Gedeeltel. gepubliceerd in T.N.I. 1852 & 1853. *I.*

Corpus Diplomaticum Neerlando-Indicum, 1e dl., uitgeg. en toegel. door J. E. Heeres (1598-1650). B.K.I. LVII 1907. *III.*

— 2e dl. uitgeg. en toegel. door J. E. Heeres (1650-1691). B.K.I. 1931. *IV.*

— 3e dl. verzameld en toegel. door F. W. Stapel (1676-1691). B.K.I. XVI 1934. *IV, V.*

Cortemünde, J. P. Dagbog fra en Ostindiefart 1672-1675, ved Henning Henningsen. Søhistoriske Skrifter, udgivet af Handels- of Søfarts-museet på Kronborg. Kronb. 1953. Vol. V. *IV.*

Couto, Diego de. Da Asia... Decada IV-XII. Lisboa 1778-1788. 10 tomos. *I, II.*

Cowan, H. K. J. Bespreking van R. A. Kern. Verbreiding van den Islâm, 9e hoofdst. der Gesch. van Ned.-Indië dl. I. Amst. 1938. Djawa XIX 1938, p. 124. *I.*

Crawfurd, J. History of the Indian Archipelago. Containing an account of the manners, arts, language, religions ... of its inhabitants. Edinburg-London 1820. 3 vols. *II.*

Crucq, K. C. De geschiedenis van het heilig kanon te Banten. T.B.G. LXXXVIII 1938, p. 359. *I.*

— De kanonnen in den Kraton te Soerakarta. T.B.G. LXXXVIII 1939, p. 9. *III.*

Daghregister gehouden in 't Casteel Batavia ... 1624-1682. Bat.-'s-Hage 1887-1931. 31 dln. Uitg. K.B.G.
De onuitgegeven delen 1683 en vlg. bevinden zich in het Arsip Negara te Jakarta. *I-VIII.*

Dam, P. van. Beschrijvinge van de Oost-Indische Compagnie, uitgeg. door F. W. Stapel. 's-Grav. 1927-1943. 5 dln. Uitg. Rijks Geschiedk. Publ. *III-V.*

Damar Woelan (Serat), awit djoemenengipoen Praboe Kenya Mahospati ngantos doemoegi Damar Woelan ... Samarang 1899. *I.*

Dapperen, J. W. van. Moeloeddagen te Cheribon. Djawa XIII 1933, p. 140. *I.*

Delplace, D. Selectae Indiarum Epistolae nunc primum editae. Florentiae 1887. *I.*

Deventer, M. L. van. Geschiedenis der Nederlanders op Java. Dl. I. Haarlem 1886. *III, VIII.*

Dijk, L. C. D. van. Neêrland's vroegste betrekkingen met Borneo ... Amst. 1862. *III.*

Djajadiningrat, Hoesein. Hari Lahirnya Djajakarta. Bahasa dan Budaya V,1. *I.*

— Critische Beschouwing van de Sadjarah Bantĕn. Bijdrage ter kenschetsing van de Jav. geschiedschrijving. Haarlem 1913. Proefschr. *I-IV.*

— Kantteekening bij "Het Javaanse Rijk Tjerbon in de eerste eeuwen van zijn bestaan" van R. A. Kern. (B.K.I. CXIII 1957, p. 191) B.K.I. CXIII 1957, p. 380. *I.*

— De naam van den eersten Mohammedaanschen Vorst in West-Java. T.B.G. LXXXII, p. 401. *I.*

Domis, H. J. Aanteekeningen, 2e-4e stukje. Pasoeroean 1829-1830. *I, V.*

Doorenbos, J. De geschriften van Hamzah Pansoeri, uitgeg. en toegel. Leiden 1933. Proefschr. *I.*

Drewes, G. W. J. New Light on the coming of Islam to Indonesia. B.K.I. CXXIV 1968, p. 433.

— Mysticism and Activism. In: Unity and Variety in Muslim Civilization, edited by G. E. von Grünebaum, Chicago 1955. *I.*

— Sech Joesoep Makasar. Djawa 1926, p. 83. *IV.*

— The Struggle between Javanism and Islam as illustrated by the Serat Dermagandul. B.K.I. CXXII 1966, p. 309. *I.*

— see Admonitions.

Edel, J. Hikayat Hasanuddin. Meppel 1938. Proefschr. *I, II.*

Erkelens, B. De geschiedenis van het rijk Gowa. Verh. K.B.G. L 3e st. 1897. *V.*

Faber, G. H. von. Oud Soerabaia. De Geschiedenis van Indië's eerste koopstad ... (Soerabaia 1931). *III-V.*

Factories (The English) in India ... A Calendar of Documents in the India Office, British Museum and Public Records Office 1618-... By Will. Foster. Oxford 1906 etc. *III.*

Filet, P. W. De verhouding der Vorsten op Java tot de Ned.-Ind. Regeering. 's-Grav. 1895. Proefschr. *II.*

Fruin-Mees, W. Waarom Batavia en Mataram van 1629-1646 geen vrede hebben gesloten. T.B.G. LXVI 1926, p. 156. *III.*

— Geschiedenis van Java dl. II. De Mohammedaansche Rijken tot de bevestiging van de macht der Compagnie. 2e herz. dr. Welt. 1925. Uitg. Volkslectuur. *II, III.*

Fruin-Mees, W. Pieter Franssen's Journaal van zijn reis naar Mataram in 1630 en eenige wegen naar de Hoofdplaats. T.B.G. LVI 1926, p. 395. *III.*

— Winrick Kieft en zijn rapport over zijn gezantschap naar Mataram in 1655. T.B.G. LXXII 1932, p. 391. *IV.*

Gericke, J. F. C. en *Roorda,* I. Javaansch-Nederlandsch Handwoordenboek. 2 dln. Amst.-Leiden 1901. *IV.*

Geschiedenis van het Madoereesche Vorstenhuis, uit het Jav. vert. door W. Palmer van den Broek. T.B.G. XX 1871, p. 241. *I, IV.*

Gijsels, Artus. Verhaal van eenige Oorlogen in Indië. Uit het Archief van Hilten. Kroniek v.h. Hist. Gen. te Utrecht. XVII 1871. Utrecht 1872, pp. 497 en 583. *II, III.*

— Grondig verhaal van Amboyna 1621. Uit het Archief v. Hilten. Kroniek v.h. Hist. Gen. te Utrecht. XVII 1871, p. 358. *II.*

Goens, Rijklof van. De vijf Gezantschapsreizen naar het Hof van Mataram 1648-54. Uitgeg. door H. J. de Graaf. 's-Grav. 1956. Linschoten Vereeniging LIX. *III, V.*

— Reijsbeschrijving van den weg uijt Samarang nae ... Mataram (en) Corte Beschrijving van 't Eijland Java ... B.K.I. IV 1856, pp. 307 and 351. *II-IV.*

Graaf, H. J. de. Bespreking van Soemarsaid Moertono's State and Statecraft in Old Java. B.K.I. CXXV 1963, p. 393. *I, III, V.*

— De historische betrouwbaarheid der Javaanse overlevering. B.K.I. CXII 1956, p. 55. *III.*

— Geschiedenis van Indonesië. 's-Grav.-Bandung 1949. *I-V.*

— Gevangenneming en Dood van raden Truna-Djaja. 26 Dec. 1679-2 Jan. 1680. T.B.G. 1952, p. 273. *IV, V.*

— Gusti Pandji Sakti. T.B.G. LXXXIII 1949, p. 59. *I, IV.*

— De Herkomst van de Kaapse "Chalifah". Tydskrif vir Wetenskap en Kuns. 1950, p. 112. *IV.*

— Het Kadjoran-vraagstuk. Djawa XX 1940, p. 273. *I, III, V.*

— Over de Kroon van Madja-Pait. B.K.I. CIX 1948, p. 573. *V.*

— Lombok in de 17e eeuw. Djawa XXI 1941. *V.*

— De Moord op kapitein François Tack. 8 febr. 1686. Amst. 1935. Proefschr.

— De Moskee van Japara. Djawa XVI 1936, p. 160. *I.*

— De Oorsprong der Javaanse Moskee. Indonesië I 1947-48, p. 289. *I, IV.*

— De Opkomst van raden Truna-Djaja. Djawa XX 1940. p. 56. *IV, V.*

— The Origin of the Javanese Mosque. Journal South-East Asian Society. Singapore IV 1963. *I.*

— De Regering van panembahan Sénapati Ingalaga. 's-Grav. 1954. Verh. K.I. XIII.

Graaf, H. J. de. De Regering van sultan Agung, vorst van Mataram. 1613-1646, en die van zijn voorganger panembahan Séda-ing-Krapjak. 1601-1613. 's-Grav. 1958. Verh. K.I. XXIII. *I, V.*

— H. J. de. De Regering van sunan Mangku-Rat I Tegal-Wangi, vorst van Mataram. 1646-1677. 2 dln. 's-Grav. 1961-1962. I. De Ontbinding van het Rijk. II. Opstand en Ondergang. Verh. K.I. XXXIII, XXXIX.

— De Reis van Mangku-Rat IV naar Mataram. T.B.G. LXXXII 1949, p. 340. *II, III.*

— Soerabaja in de XVIIe eeuw. Djawa XXI 1941, p. 199. *III-V.*

— Titels en namen van Javaanse vorsten en groten uit de 16e en 17e eeuw. B.K.I. CIX 1953, p. 62. *III-V.*

— Tomé Pires' "Suma Oriental" en het Tijdperk van Godsdienstovergang op Java. B.K.I. CVIII 1952, p. 132. *I, III.*

— De eerste nauwkeurig gedateerde uitbarsting van de Merapi, 4 aug. 1672. Djawa XX 1940, p. 122. *IV.*

— De Vlucht van Amangkoerat Tegalwangi ... T.B.G. LXXXI 1941, p. 189. *IV.*

— en *Pigeaud,* Th. G. Th. De eerste Moslimse vorstendommen op Java. Studiën over de staatkundige geschiedenis van de 15de en 16de eeuw. 's-Grav. 1974. Verh. K.I. 69. *IX.*

Graaff, Nic. de. Reisen gedaan naar alle gewesten des Werelds ... Uitgeg. door J. C. Warnsinck. 's-Grav. 1930 L.V. XXXIII. *VIII.*

Groeneveldt, W. F. Notes on the Malay Archipelago and Malacca compiled from Chinese Sources. Bat. 1877. Verh. K.B.G. XXXIX dl. 1. *I.*

Groneman, J. D. De Garebegs te Ngajogyakarta. Met photogrammen van (K.) Cephas. 's-Grav. 1895. Uitg. K.I. *I.*

Grünebaum, G. E. v. Unity and Variety in Muslim Civilization. Chicago 1955. *I.*

Haan, F. de. Priangan. De Preanger-Regentschappen onder het Nederlandsche Bestuur ... Bat. 1910-1912. 4 dln. Uitg. K.B.G. *I-V.*

Hageman JCzn., J. Algemeene Geschiedenis van Java van de vroegste tijden af aan tot op onze dagen. Indisch Archief ... 1e en 2e jaarg. dl. I-IV 1850-1851. *I, III.*

— Handleiding tot de kennis der geschiedenis, aardrijkskunde, fabelleer en tijdrekenkunde van Java. Bat. 1852. 2 dln. *I-III, VIII.*

Heekeren, H. R. v. The Bronze-Iron Age of Indonesia. 's-Grav. 1958. Verh. K.I. XXII. *I.*

Hikajat Bandjar. A Study in Malay Historiography. Proefschr. .... door J. J. Ras. 's-Grav. (1968). Bibliotheca Indonesica 1. *I.*

Hikayat Patani, edited and translated by A. Teeuw and D. K. Wyatt. Leiden 1970. 2 dln. Bibliotheca Indonesica 5. *I.*

Hoëvell, W. R. van. Reis over Java, Madoera en Bali in . . . 1847. Uitgeg. onder toezigt van P. J. Veth. Amsterdam 1849-1854. 3 dln. *II*.

Hofdijk, W. J. In 't harte van Java. Amst. 1881. *IV*.

Holle, K. F. Bijdragen tot de geschiedenis der Preanger Regentschappen. T.B.G. XVII 1869, p. 310. *III, V*.

— Een Pijagem van den Vorst van Mataram. T.B.G. XIII 1864. *III, IV*.

Hoorn, Joan van (?). Corte Beschrijving van het NoordOostelijkste gedeelte van Java, opkomst en voortgang. Notitiën rakende Java's Oostkust. (Bat. ± 1700-1703). Ms. K.I. no. H 73. *I, II, IV*.

Horst, H. van der. Oospronk van de eerste Heerschappije van de Jav. Regeeringen op het Eijland Groot-Java, opgesteld uijt de oude Jav. geschriften ende verhaalen. Biang-Lala, Ind. Leeskabinet IV dl. 1. Bat. 1855, p. 262. *II*.

Huet, Cd. Busken. Het Land van Rembrandt. Studiën over de Noord-Nederlandsche Beschaving in de 17e eeuw. 2e dl. Haarlem 1884. *V*.

Iongh, D. de. Het Krijgswezen onder de O.I. Compagnie, Den Haag 1952. *V*.

Jacobs, H. Th. Th. M. A Treatise of the Moluccos (ca. 1554). Probably the preliminary Version of Antonio Galvão's lost Histório das Moluccas. Edited, annotated and translated . . . Ms. in the Archivo Gen. de Indias. Rome-St. Louis 1971. Sources and Studies for the Hist. of the Jesuits, vol. III. *I*.

Jasper, J. E. Geschiedenis van Toeban. Met Regentenlijst en Schetskaart van de Begraafplaats Sentana (met de begraafplaats van Soenan Bonang). Tijdschr. voor het B.B. LII 1917, p. 308. *I, II*.

— Het Stadje Koedoes en zijn oude Kunst. Ned.-Indië Oud en Nieuw 1922, p. 1.*V*.

— en *Pirngadie* (Mas). De Inlandsche Kunstnijverheid in Ned.-Indië. I. Het Vlechtwerk, 's-Grav. 1912. III. De Batikkunst, 's-Grav. 1916. IV. De Goud- en Zilversmeedkunst. 's-Grav. 1927. *VIII*.

J.D.V. Bijdragen tot de Kennis van de residentie Madioen. T.N.I. XVII 1855, p. 13. *I*.

Johns, A. H. Mystics and Historical Writing. In: Historians of S.E. Asia. Edited by D. G. W. Hall. London-New York-Toronto 1961. *I*.

Junghuhn, Franz. Java, seine Gestalt, Pflanzendecke und innere Bauart . . . in 's Deutsche übertragen von J. K. Hasskarl. 3 Abtn. Leipzig 1852-1854. *V*.

Juynboll, Th. W. Handleiding tot de Kennis van de Mohammedaansche Wet volgens de Sjāficitische School. Leiden 1903. *I*.

Kanda, see Serat Kanda.

Karta Soedirdja, Tjareta Naghara Songĕnnĕp. In: Eerste Congres voor de Taal-, Land- en Volkenkunde van Java. Soerakarta 24-26 dec. 1920, p. 361. *I.*

Kartini, raden adjeng-. Door Duisternis tot Licht. Gedachten over en voor het Javaansche Volk, met inleiding door J. H. Abendanon. Semarang-Soerabaja-'s-Grav. 1911. *I-III.*

Kern. R. A. Het Javaanse rijk Tjĕrbon in de eerste eeuwen van zijn bestaan. B.K.I. CXIII 1957, p. 191. *I.*

— De Verbreiding van den Islam. In: Geschiedenis v. Ned.-Indië, onder leiding van F. W. Stapel. Dl. I. Amst. 1938, p. 299. *I, II.*

Kidung Pamancangah. De Geschiedenis van het rijk Gèlgèl, critisch uitgeg. door C. C. Berg. Santpoort 1929. Jav.-Balische hist. geschriften no. 1. Uitg. Kirtya Liefrinck-v. d. Tuuk. *I.*

Klinkert, H. C. Nieuw Maleisch-Nederlandsch Woordenboek met Arabisch karakter naar de beste bronnen bewerkt. Leiden 1893. *I.*

Knoop, W. J. Krijgs- en geschiedkundige Beschouwingen over Willem den derde. 1e dl. (1672-1673). Schiedam 1895. *V.*

Kock, A. H. W. de. Korte chronologische Geschiedenis van Palembang. Tijdschr. v. N.I. VIII 1846. *I.*

Koentjaraningrat. Additional information on the Kenthols of South Central Java. Madjalah Ilmu Sastra Indonesia II 1964. *I.*

Kraemer, H. Mededeelingen over den Islam op Ambon en Haroekoe. Djawa VII 1927, p. 77. *I.*

Kroeskamp, H. De Westkust en Menangkabau (1665-1668). Utr. 1931. Proefschr. *I, IV.*

Krom, N. J. Hindoe-Javaansche Geschiedenis. 2e herz. dr. 's-Grav. 1931. Uitg. K.I. *I-III, V.*

— Inleiding tot de Hindoe-Javaansche Kunst. 2e herz. dr. 's-Grav. 1923. 3 dln. *II, III, V.*

— Het jaar van den val van Madjapahit. T.B.G. LV 1913, p. 232. *I.*

Kronijk van Palembang. Hs. v.h. K.I. H 371 (vertaling v.h. Mal. hs. no. 414). *I.*

Kunst, J. De Toonkunst van Java. 2 dln. 's-Grav. 1934. *VIII.*

Leemans, C. Jav. tempels bij Prambanan. B.K.I. 1855, p. 1. *III, IV.*

Lekkerkerker, C. Bali en Lombok. Overzicht der litteratuur ... Rijswijk 1920. Uitg. Bali-Instituut. *III.*

Leupe, P. A. Het Gezantschap onder den G.G. H. Brouwer naar Bali in 1833. B.K.I. V 1856, p. 1. *III.*

— Stukken betrekkelijk het Beleg en de Verovering van Malakka 1640-1641. Berichten Hist. Gen. te Utrecht 1862. *III.*

Livros das Monções. Arquivo Nacional da Torre do Tombo, Lissabon. (± 1725). *III.*

Louw, P. J. F. De Java-oorlog van 1825 tot 1830. Uitgeg. door het K.B.G. met medewerking van de Ned. Indische Regeering. Dl. I. Batavia-'s-Hage 1894. *IV*.

Mac Leod, N. De Oost-Indische Compagnie als Zeemogendheid in Azië. Rijswijk 1927. 2 dln. *III*.

Malaiische Weisheit und Geschichte. Einführung in die malaiische Literatur. Die Krone aller Fürsten, die Chronik der Malaien. Aus dem Malaiischen übertragen von H. Overbeck. Jena 1927. *I*.

Maronier, J. H. Pictures of the Tropics. A Catalogue. 's-Grav. 1967. Uitg. K.I. *I*.

Mason, A. E. W. The Life of Francis Drake. London 1941. *II*.

Mayer, E. Th. Een Blik in het Jav. Volksleven. Leiden 1897. 2 dln. *I, V*.

— Vier Jav. Legenden uit de Residentie Madioen medegedeeld. B.K.I. XLII 1893, p. 45. *I*.

Mees, C. A. De Kroniek van Koetai. Tekstuitgave met toelichting. Santpoort 1935. Proefschr. *I*.

Meilink-Roelofsz, M. A. F. Asian Trade and European Influence in the Indonesian Archipelago between 1500 and about 1630. 's-Grav. 1962. Proefschr. *I*.

Moens, J. Çrivijaya, Iava en Kataha. T.B.G. LXXVII 1937, p. 317. *I*.

Mohammedaansche Oudheden in en om Grissee op Java. Naar Jav. origineele stukken getrouw nageteekend door A. van Pers en geannoteerd door (J.) Hageman (JCzn.). Uit de tekeningenverz. van het K.I. K 16. *I*.

Muller, G. Proeve eener Geschiedenis van een gedeelte der Westkust van Borneo. Indische Bij 1843 I, p. 321. *I*.

Muntinghe, H. W. Acte van Vreede, Vriend- en Bondgenootschap aangegaan en gesloten tusschen H. W. Muntinghe ... en Mahometh Badaroedin, gew. sultan van Palembang ... Palembang 1818. Hs. K.I. H 173. *I*.

Naber, S. P. l'Honoré. In een open sloep van Australië naar Java. Marineblad XXV 1910-11, p. 18. *III*.

— De derde Voijagie van G. Hoeq naer Oost-Indië. Marineblad XXV 1910-11, pp. 193, 289, 422, 533. *III*.

Navarrete, M. F. de. Colecion de los Viages y Descubriementos que hizeron los marinos Españoles.

Neyens, M. De geheimzinnige Klok. T.B.G. LXXVI 1930, p. 81. *II*.

Noorduyn, J. Een achttiende-eeuwse Kroniek van Wadjo'. Buginese Historiografie. 's-Grav. 1955. Proefschr.

— De Islamisering van Makassar. B.K.I. CXII 1956, p. 247. *IV*.

— Further topographical Notes on the Ferry Charter of 1358. With appendices on Djipang and Bodjanegara. B.K.I. CXXIV 1968, p. 460. *V*.

Noort, Olivier v. De Reis om de Wereld 1598-1601. Met inleid. en aanteek. uitgeg. door J. W. IJzerman. 's-Grav. 1926. 2 dln. Uitg. Linschoten Vereeniging XXVII-XXVIII. *III*.

Nüsselein, A. H. P. J. Beschrijving van het landschap Pasir. B.K.I. LVIII 1905, p. 532. *III*.

Oudheidkundig Verslag 1930. Uitg. K.B.G. Bat. 1931, p. 52-57. (Verslag over de Oudheden te Mantingan, met illustraties). *I, II*.

Opkomst (De) *van het Nederlandsche Gezag* in Oost-Indië. Verzameling van onuitgegeven stukken uit het Kol. Archief. Uitgeg. en bew. door J. K. J. de Jonge ... dl. I-X. 's-Grav.-Amst. 1862-1875. *III-VIII*.

Overbeck, H., see Malaiische Weisheit.

Padma Susastra. Rangsang Tuban. Surakarta 1900. *I*.

— Sejarah Dalem pangiwa lan panengen. Semarang-Surabaya 1902. *I-IV*.

Pa'Kamar. Geschiedenis van Madoera. Djawa VI 1926, p. 231. *I*.

Palmer van den Broek, W. Geschiedenis van het Vorstenhuis van Madoera, uit het Jav. vertaald. T.B.G. XX 1873, p. 241 and p. 471. *I*.

Pandjenongan ing Kaboepatèn Soera Pringga. Ms. K.B.G. Brandes 474. *I*.

Pararaton (Kèn Angrok) of het Boek der Koningen van Tumapĕl en van Majapahit, uitgeg. en toegel. door J. L. A. Brandes. 2e dr. bew. door N. J. Krom. 's-Grav.-Bat. 1920. Verh. K.B.G. LXII 1920. *I*.

Parlindungan, Pongkinangolngolan Sinambela gelar Tuangku Rao ... 1816-1833 [Djakarta 1964]. *I*.

Pigafetta, Antonio, Relazione di — sul primo Viaggio intorno al Globo... Roma 1894. *I*.

Pigeaud, Th. G. Th. Aanteekeningen betreffende den Jav. Oosthoek. T.B.G. LXXII 1932, p. 215. *III*.

— Alexander, Sakèndèr en Sénapati. Djawa VII 1927, p. 321. *I-III*.

— Jav. Beschavingsgesch. 3 dln. Hs. K.I. no. H 717 a-c: a. Ontwerpen en Overzichten. b. I. Het uiterlijk der Beschaving. c. III. Geloof en Godsdienst. *I*.

— Catalogue raisonné of Jav. Manuscripts in the Library of the University of Leiden and other Collections in the Netherlands. 3 vols. Leiden 1967-1970. I. Synopsis of Jav. Literature, II. Descriptive Lists of Jav. Manuscripts, III. Illustrations and Facsimiles ... Maps. Addenda and a general Index. Bibliotheca Universitatis Leidensis. Codices Manuscripti IX-XI. *I*.

— Jav. Volksvertoningen. Bijdrage tot de Beschrijving van Land en Volk. Bat. 1938. Uitg. Volkslectuur. *I-IV*.

Pigeaud, Th. G. Th. Java in the 14th century, a Study in Cultural History. The Nāgara-Kertāgama by Rakawi Prapanca of Majapahit 1365 A.D. 3d ed., revised and enlarged by some contemporaneous texts, with notes, translations, commentaries and a recapitulation. 5 vols. The Hague 1962-1963. IV. Commentaries and Recapitulation, V. Glossary and General Index. Uitg. K.I. Translation Series 4, 4-5. *I*.

— Tantu Panggelaran. Een Oud-Jav. Prozageschrift, uitgeg., vertaald en toegel. 's-Grav. 1924. Proefschr. *I*.

Pijper, G. F. The Minaret in Java. India Antiqua, p. 274. *III*.

Pinto, Fern. Mendes. Peregrinação . . . Nova Edição conforme à primeira de 1614. Lisboa 1829. 3 tomos. *I-III, V*.

— Les Voyages Aventureux. Trad. du Portugais par B. Figuier. T. 3e. Paris 1830. *I-III, V*.

Pires, Tomé. Suma Oriental, edited and translated by Armando Cortesão. London 1944. 2 vols. Hakluyt Society, secd. Series nos. LXXXIX & XC. *I, II*.

Poel, A. v. d. De Oorsprong van den naam Bagelèn en het aldaar gevestigde Geslacht der Kèntols. T.N.I. VIII 1846, p. 173. *I*.

Poensen, G. Mangkubumi, Ngajogjakarta's eerste Sultan (n.a.v. een Jav. handschrift). B. K. I. LI 1901, p. 223. *II*.

Poerbatjaraka, rd. mas ng. Pandji-verhalen onderling vergeleken. Bandoeng 1940. Bibliotheca Javanica. Uitg. K.B.G. *II*.

— Ménak, Beschrijving der handschriften. K.B.G. Bandoeng 1940. *I*.

Poerwa Soewignja (R.) and *Wira Wangsa* (R.). Pratélan kawontenan ing buku-buku Djawa tjitakan . . . ing Museum . . . Genootschap ing Betawi. Bat. 1921. Jav. bibliographie gegrond op de boekwerken in die taal, aanwezig in de boekerij van het (K.)B.G. Met een voorbericht van D. A. Rinkes. Bat. 1920-21. 2 dln. *I*.

Pranatjitra, een Jav. Liefde. Uit het Jav. vert. door C. C. Berg, met medew. van M. Prawira-atmadja. Santpoort 1930. *III*.

Prawirawinarsa (rd.) and *Djajengpranata* (rd. arya). I. Babad Alit . . . Welt. 1921. Volkslectuur serie no. 462. *I-IV*.

Prijono. Sri Tanjung. Een oud Jav. Verhaal. Leiden 1938. Proefschr. *I*.

Prins, J. Indische Gedichten. Bijeengebr. n.a.v. de Tentoonstelling Ned.-Indië in de Letterkunde, gehouden te 's-Grav. Haarlem 1932. *IV*.

Raffles, Th. St. The History of Java. London 1817. 2 vols. *I, IV*.

Rapporten van de Commissie in Ned.-Indië *voor Oudheidkundig Onderzoek* op Java en Madoera. 1910. Bat.-'s-Grav. 1911. Uitg. K.B.G. *II*.

Rassers, W. H. Çiwa en Boeddha in den Indischen Archipel. Gedenkschrift K.I. 1926. *I.*

Rees, W. v. Toontje Poland. Rotterdam 1896. *III.*

Rijali. Hikayat Tanah Hitu. Codex 8756 der L.U.B. Malay. *I.*

Rinkes, D. A. Abdoerraoef van Singkel. Bijdrage tot de kennis van de Mystiek op Sumatra en Java. Heerenveen 1909. Proefschr. *I.*

— Een Jav. Genoveva. Codex LOr. 8598-B L.U.B. coll. Rinkes. *I.*

— De Heiligen van Java I-VI. T.B.G. LII-LV 1910-1913. *I-III.*

Romondt, V. R. van. De Oudheden van de Penanggungan. Jakarta 1951. Hs. K.I. no. H 655. Vertaling der inleiding op de uitgave van de Dines Purbakala Republik Indonesia: Peninggalan2 purbakala di Gunung Penanggungan. *I.*

Roo de la Faille, P. de. Studie over Lomboksch Adatrecht. Adatrechtbundel no. XV, p. 131. Bali en Lombok. *I, II, IV.*

— Uit den Palembangschen Sultanstijd. Feestbundel K.B.G. Bat. 1928 dl. II, p. 316. *I, II, IV.*

Rouffaer, G. P. Genealogische gegevens over de Vorsten en onafhankelijke Prinsen van Java. Ms. K.I. no. H 767. *IV.*

— Wanneer is Madjapahit gevallen? Het Tijdperk van Godsdienstovergang (1400-1600) in den Maleischen Archipel. B.K.I. L 1899, p. 111. *I, II.*

— Was Malaka Emporium vóór 1400 A.D. genaamd Malajoer... B.K.I. LXXVII 1921, p. 1.

— Padjang. Artikel in Encyclopaedie van N.I. 2e dr. 's-Grav.-Leiden 1919. dl. III, p. 244. *I, II.*

— Eene duistere plaats over Java's staatkundige toestand tijdens Padjang in 1580 opgehelderd. Album Kern 1903, p. 267. *II.*

— Encyclopaedie-artikelen (oorspronkelijk bestemd voor de 2e dr. der Encyclopaedie v. Ned.-Indië). B.K.I. 1930. LXXXVI, p. 191. *I.*

— Tenggereezen. Artikel in Encyclopaedie van N.I. 2e dr. 's-Grav.-Leiden 1920. dl. IV, p. 298. *III.*

— Voorwoord bij: De val van de kraton van Padjang door toedoen van Sénapati (± 1586), volgens de Babad Tanah Djawi. B.K.I. L 1899, p. 284. *II.*

— Vorstenlanden. Overdruk uit Adatrechtbundel XXXIV Serie D. no. 81, p. 233-378. 's-Grav. 1931. Idem in Encyclopaedie van Ned.-Indië 1e dr. dl. IV, p. 587. *IV, V.*

Roux, C. C. F. M. le. Twee Portugese plattegronden van Oud Batavia uit den stichtingstijd der Stad. T.B.G. LXXVIII 1938. *III.*

Roy, J. Jansz. de. Voyagie gedaan ... na Borneo en Atchin in ... 1691. (Amst. 1700?) *I.*

Rumphius, G. E. De Ambonse Historie. Behelsende een kort Verhaal der Gedenkwaardigste Geschiedenissen ... voorgevallen sedert dat de Ned. O.I. Comp. het besit in Amboina gehadt heeft. B.K.I. LXIV 1910. 2dln. in 1 band. *III, IV*.

Sajarah Melayu (die Chronik der Malaien) in: Malaiische Weisheit und Geschichte. Einführung in die Malaiische Literatur ... Aus dem Malaiischen übertragen von Hans Overbeck. Jena 1927. *I*.

Sajarah Regèn Surabaya. Ms. K.B.G. coll. Br. no. 474. *I-V*.

Sedjarah Melayu, menurut terbitan Abdullah ibn Abdul Kadir Munsji. Diselenggarakan kembali dan diberi anotasi oleh T. D. Situmorang dan A. Teeuw dengan bantuan Amal Hamzah. Djakarta-Amst. 1952. *I*.

Salasilah ing para Luluhur ing Kadanuredjan. Coll. Pigeaud LOr. 6685 L.U.B. *I*.

Salokantara, lawbook, Ms. Leiden, Catalogue Pigeaud, vol. I, p. 308. *I*.

Sarkar, Sadunath. Shivaji and his Times. Calcutta 1920. *III*.

Schipvaert (De eerste) der Nederlanders naar Oost-Indië onder Cornelis de Houtman 1595-1597. Dl. I-II. 's-Grav. 1915-1925. Uitg. Linschoten Vereeniging XII, XXV. *I, III*.

Schipvaert (De tweede) der Nederlanders naar Oost-Indië onder J. van Neck en W. Warwijck. 1598-1600. 's-Grav. 1953. Uitg. Linschoten Vereeniging LIII. *I-III*.

Schnitger, F. W. Archaeology of Hindoo Sumatra. Internat. Archiv. für Ethnographie. Supplement dl. XXXV 1937. *I*.

Schoel, W. F. Alphabetisch Register van de administratieve ... en adatrechtelijke indeeling van Ned.-Indië. Dl. I: Java en Madoera. Welt. 1931. *II-V*.

Schouten, W. Oost-Indische voyagie ... Amst. 1675. 2 dln. *IV*.

Schrieke, B. J. O. Het Boek van Bonang. Utr. 1916. Proefschr. *I*.

— Prolegomena tot eene sociologische studie over de Volken van Sumatra. T.B.G. LXI 1925, p. 90. *I*.

— Ruler and Realm in early Java. Indonesian Sociological Studies. Selected Writings. The Hague-Bandung 1955. Studies by Dutch scholars on Indonesia no. 2. *I*.

Schurhammer S.J., Georg. Die zeitgenossischen Quellen zur Geschichte Portugiesisch-Asiens und seiner Nachbarländer ... zur zeit des Hl. Franz Xaver (1538-1552) ... Leipzig 1932. Veröffentlichungen der Katholischen Universität Jôchi Daigaku, Tôkyô. Xaveriusreihe Bd. I. *I*.

Serat Kanda. Ned. vert., beginnende met ... Adji Saka. 4 dln. ms. K.B.G. no. 54. *I-IV*.

Serat Kandaning Ringgit Purwa. Ms. LOr. 6379 L.U.B. (afschr. cod. K.B.G. no. 7). *I-IV*.

Serat Tjabolang en Serat Tjentini Inhoudsopgaven bewerkt door Th. Pigeaud. Verh. K.B.G. LXXIII 1933 2e st. *III*.

Serrurier, H. De Wajang Poerwa. Eene ethnologische studie. Leiden 1896. 2 dln. *I, III*.

Singodimedjo, Kasman. Geschiedenis en lotsbestel der desa Windoeadji naar het volksgeloof (een stukje desa-psychologie). Kol. Studiën 1941, p. 44.

Snouck Hurgronje, C. The Achehnese. Translated by ... A. W. S. O'Sullivan ... Leyden 1906. 2 vols. *I*.

— De Atjehers. Uitgeg. op last der Regeering. Bat.-Leiden 1893-1894. 2 dln. *I*.

— Mr. L. W. C. van den Berg's beoefening van het Mohammedaansche Recht. Verspr. Geschriften II. Bonn-Leipzig 1923, p. 59. *I*.

— Mekka ... herausgegeben von "Het K.I.T.L.V." Haag 1888-1889. 2 Bände. *I*.

Soedjono Tirtokoesoemo. De Besaran der Regentschapshoofdplaats te Demak. Djawa XVII 1937, p. 133. *I*.

Soegriwa, I Gusti Bagus. Sedjarah Arja Tabanan. Ms. Kirtya Liefrinck-v. d. Tuuk; also K.I., ms. Or. 487. (Dutch transl. ± 1950).

Soehari, S. Pinggirs. Djawa IX 1929, p. 160. *III*.

Soemarsaid Moertono. State and Statecraft in old Java. A Study of the later Mataram Period, 16th to 19th century. Ithaca N.Y. 1968. S.E.A. Program Dept. of Asian Studies, Cornell University. Monograph Series. Modern Indonesia Project. *III, IV*.

Soema Sentika. De Geschiedenis van het Rijk Kědiri, opgeteekend in ... 1873, van aanteekeningen en eene vertal. voorzien en uitgeg. door P. W. van den Broek. Leiden 1902. *V*.

Soerja Nagara, pg. aria. Babad Sengakalaning Momana. Hs. K.B.G. also K.I., ms. Or. 257. *I-IV*.

Soewignja. Kjai Ageng Pandhanarang. Bat. 1938. Uitg. Balé Pustaka serie no. 1271. *I*.

Solichin Salam. Sunan Kudus, Riwajat hidup serta perdjoangannya. Penerbit Menara. Kudus 1959. *I, V*.

Speelman, Corn. Notitie ... tot naarrigtingen van ... Jan van den Oppijnen ... Opperhoofd, en van den Cap. Jan Franz. ... anno 1669. Ms. in Arsip Negara te Djakarta en Rijks Archief in den Haag. *IV*.

Stapel, F. W. Het Bongaais Verdrag. De Vestiging der Nederlanders op Makassar. Gron.-den Haag 1922. Proefschr. *IV, V*.

— Cornelis Janszoon Speelman. 's-Grav. 1936. *IV, V*.

Stein-Callenfels, P. V. van, *Vuuren*, L. van. Bijdragen tot de Topografie van de Residentie Soerabaja in de 14e eeuw. Tijdschr. Kon. Ned. Aardrijksk. Gen. XLI 1924. *I.*

— Suda Mala en de Hindu-Javaansche Kunst. Verh. K.B.G. LXVI 1925 le st. *I.*

Sturler, W. L. de (?). Beknopte chronologische aanteekening van de Vorsten, die over Palembang hebben geheerscht, met vermelding ... van hunne namen en verdeelinge, verwantschap ... Hs. K.I. no. H 371a. *I.*

Stutterheim, W. F. Leerboek der Ind. Cultuurgesch. II & III. Gron.-den Haag-Bat. 1932. II. Het Hinduïsme in den Archipel. III. De Islam en zijn Komst in den Archipel. *I.*

— A Javanese Period in Sumatran History. Surakarta 1929. *II.*

— De Kraton van Majapahit. Verh. K.I. VII 1949. *II, III.*

— Een vrij Overzetveer te Wanagiri (M.N.) in 903 A.D. T.B.G. LXXIV 1934, p. 269. *I.*

S. Wardi. Kumpulan Tjeritera lama dari Kota Wali. Demak z.j. *I.*

Tiele, P. De Europeërs in den Maleischen Archipel I-IX. 's-Grav. 1877-1887. Uit B.K.I. 4e reeks I - 5e reeks II. *I, III.*

Tjabolang, see Serat Tjabolang.

Tjandrapradata, rd. ng. Serat Tjandrakanta. Pangimpoenipoen - - - djil. I. Soerakarta 1923. *IV, VII.*

Transscriptie van het Dagboek der Vorsten van *Gowa* en *Tello*, met vertal. en aantn. door K. Ligtvoet. B.K.I. XXVIII 1889. *III-V.*

Troostenburg de Bruijn, C. A. L. Biographisch Woordenboek van Oost-Indische Predikanten. Nijmegen 1893. *V.*

Tuuk, H. N. van der. Kawi-Balineesch-Nederlandsch Woordenboek, uitgeg. door J. Brandes. Bat. 1897-1902. 4 dln. *I.*

Uhlenbeck, E. M. A critical Survey of Studies on the Languages of Java and Madura. 's-Grav. Bibliographical Series K.I. no. 7. *I.*

Valentijn, François. Oud en Nieuw Oost-Indiën. Dordrecht-Amst. 1724-1726. 5 dln. in 8 bdn. *I-VI.*

— Oud en Nieuw Oost-Indiën. Met aanteekeningen ... inhoudsregisters, chronologische lijsten enz. Uitgeg. door S. Keijzer. 2e uitg. Amst. 1862. 3 dln. *VII, VIII.*

Veld, S. G. in 't. Ontstaan van het vorstendom Pasir, Oostkust van Borneo. T.B.G. XXVI 1882, p. 557. *I.*

Verbeek, R. D. M. and *Fennema*, R. Geologische Beschrijving van Java en Madoera. Amst. 1896. 2 dln. *V.*

Veth, P. Java... historisch. 2e dr. I. Oude Geschiedenis, II. Nieuwe Geschiedenis. Haarlem 1898. 2 dln. *II, III.*

— Nalezingen en Verbeteringen op het 3e deel van "Java". Tijdschr. v.h. Kon. Ned. Aardrijksk. Gen. VI 1882, p. 82. *I.*

— Uit Oost en West. Verklaring van eenige uitheemsche woorden, Arnhem 1889. *V.*

Visser, B. J. J. Onder Portugeesch-Spaansche vlag. De Kath. Missie van Indonesië, 1511-1605. Amst. [1926]. *I.*

— Onder de Compagnie. Geschiedenis der Kath. Missie van Ned.-Indië. Bat. (1934). *III.*

Vreede, A.C. Catalogus van de Javaansche en Madoereesche Handschriften der L.U.B. Leiden 1892. *I.*

Wall, H. von de. Vervolg van het extract uit de dagelijksche aanteekeningen van de civiele gezaghebber van Koetei en de Oostkust van Borneo. Indisch Archief ... II 1850 iii, p. 449. *I.*

Wall, V. I. van de. De Nederlandsche Oudheden in de Molukken. 's-Grav. 1928. *V.*

Werdi-Sastra (R.) & *Sastra-Wijaya* (R.), Bhabhad Songenep. Welt. 1921, 2 dln. Uitg. Balé Pustaka nos. 342, 342a. *I, III, IV.*

Wertheim, W. F. Selected Studies on Indonesia. Indonesian economics. The Hague 1961. *I.*

Wessels, C. De eerste Franciscaner-Missie op Java (± 1584-1599). Studiën, N. reeks LXII Nijmegen 1938, dl. 113 1e halfjr., p. 117. *I, II.*

— Wat staat geschiedkundig vast over de oude Missie in Zuid-Selébès of het land van Makassar, 1525-1669? Studiën, juni 1925. *I, II.*

Wijnaents van Resandt, W. De Gezaghebbers der O.I. Compagnie op hare Buiten-Comptoiren in Azië... Amst. 1944. Genealogische Bibl. II. *V.*

Winstedt, R. O. History of Malaya. Journal of the Malayan Branch of the Royal Asiatic Society XII 1933. *I.*

Winter, C. F. Javaansche Samenspraken. 3e dr. Amst. 1882. *II, III.*

Wiselius, J. A. B. Historisch Onderzoek naar de geestelijke en wereldlijke Suprematie van Grissee op Midden- en Oost-Java gedurende de 16e en 17e eeuw. T.B.G. XXIII 1876, p. 459. *I-III.*

Wolters, O. W. Early Indonesian Commerce. Ithaca N.Y. 1967. *I.*

Zentgraaf, H. C. Atjeh. Bat. (1940). *V.*

GENERAL INDEX OF NAMES

of Indonesian, Chinese and European names found in Dr de Graaf's eight books and articles, and in the Summary, with explanatory notes. The Roman serial numbers at the end of the notes are explained in the Key (p. 105). The Arabic numerals refer to pages.

As Dr de Graaf's eight books and articles were originally written in Dutch, the Dutch transliteration system of Indonesian words was used. In the present General Index the spelling of all Javanese names and words has been modernized in accordance with the rules of orthography of Indonesian languages which are laid down by Government. (Only the ḍ, ṭ, and ĕ have been retained where it seemed convenient to do so).

Personal names of well-known Javanese scholars and authors who lived in the twentieth century, such as Djajadiningrat, have not been altered.

The sixteenth century Portuguese texts and the seventeenth and eighteenth century Dutch reports and books that have been used as sources of history contain several Indonesian names in Portuguese and Dutch transliteration which were difficult to identify. Some of them could not be made out at all. They have been put between quotation marks in the Index.

Some typical Dutch-Javanese words and expressions which are found in Dr de Graaf's texts have also been put between quotation marks, and provided with English explanations.

The following abbreviations of names and titles are used in the Index.

ad.	adipati (ruler, prince)	Mad.	Madurese
ag.	agĕng (great)	Mak.	Makasarese
Bal.	Balinese	ng.	ngabèhi (official)
Bug.	Buginese	ny.	nyahi (old, lady of standing)
Chin.	Chinese	pan.	panĕmbahan (prince)
dem.	dĕmang (officer)	pg.	pangéran (religious leader, prince)
dip.	dipati, adipati		
Jav.	Javanese	Port.	Portuguese
ker. kr.	kĕraèng (South Celebes title)	rd.	radèn (gentleman of standing)
		secr.	secretary
ky.	kyahi (old, gentleman of standing)	sult.	sultan
		Sund.	Sundanese
lieut.	lieutenant	tg.	tumĕnggung (commander)

A

Abad Sara, see Ampat Sara.
Abbas, son of Abdul Muntalip, I 282.
Abbas II, shah of Persia, IV-1 80.
Abdul (ĕncik), interpreter, V 130, 202, 213.
Abdu'l-Aziz (sayyid) from Jeddah, I 251.
Abdul Kadir, king of Banten, I 124; IX 13.
Abdul Kahar ibn Mataram (sult.), name of Sénapati, II 115.
Abdul Kalianget, Bal. soldier, V 98.
Abdullah, name of sult. Agung, III 266-268.
Abdullah (maulana), man of religion, II 81.
Abdul Latif, shahbandar of Japara, IV-1 76.
Abdul Mahometh Molany Mattarany, name of sult. Agung, III 267.
Abdul Muntalip, king of Mecca, I 282.
Abdul Rahman, sult. of Palembang, I 205, 303.
Abdul Rahman, man of religion, Tuban, ancestor, I 132, 282.
Abrahamsz. (Jan), artillerist, V 212.
Abu Hurérah, of Cempa, cousin of pg. Ngampel, I 21.
Abul Fath, Abdul Fatah, sult. of Banten, IV-1 8.
Aceh, Acheh, Achin, I 19, 22, 23, 79, 81, 112, 201, 245, 258, 266, 273; II 34, 35, 68; III 164, 165, 170, 229, 230, 268, 279; IV-1 82, 117, 196; IV-2 105; IX 5, 12, 29, 43.
Acunha (Jorge d'), Port. ambassador, III 168, 170, 171, 223-225, 228.
Adam (L.), I 254, 315; III 105; IV-1 12, 14; IV-2 8, 134; V 121, 140, 144, 149.
Adam (paté), Malay trader, father of paté Cucuf of Gresik, I 142.
"adatrecht", popular law and custom, I 67.

Adi (ratu), of Pajang, mother of sult. Agung, III 27.
Adi (sunan), son of sunan Kali Jaga, II 29, 51, 77, 79.
Adi Baya (ny. gedé), sister of ki gedé Séséla, II 5.
adikara, adikarana, Old Jav.: ruler, rule, I 132, 283.
Adikara (arya), legendary ruler of Tuban, I 283.
Adil (ratu), Jav. Islamic saviour, VII 49.
Adi Langu, see Ngadi Langu.
Adining Kusuma, name of pan. Giri Laya, IV-1 39.
Adipati (kyahi), ancient title of princes and rulers, II 38, 103; III 80.
Adipati Anom (pg.), crownprince, pan. Krapyak, II 128.
Adipati Anom (pg.), crownprince, later Mangku Rat I, III 104, 241, 286; IV-1 7.
Adipati Anom (pg.), crownprince, later Mangku Rat II, III 211; IV-1 6, 198-200, 204; IV-2 1-3, 10-12, 18, 22, 23, 25, 26, 32-38, 41, 42, 46, 47, 51-54, 56, 57, 69, 70, 80, 83, 84, 86, 88, 110, 111, 114-119, 121-127, 139, 140, 145, 146, 153-158, 179, 183-186, 188, 189, 192, 193; V 3, 61, 94; VII 10-15, 38, 50; VIII 3.
Adipati Anom (pg.), crownprince, later Mangku Rat III, V 106, 108, 124, 145, 154, 157, 158, 162-166.
Adipati Anom (pg.), kr. Galésong, IV-2 110.
Adipati Anom (pg.), ruler of Jambi, III 276, 278.
Adipati Anom (rd.), son of pg. Madyun, V 249.
Adi Prabu Anyakrawati Sénapati Ingalaga Mataram, pan. Krapyak, III 1.
Adi Purana, Old Jav. book, I 186, 297.

Adi Sara, locality, I 261.

Adi Sara (ny.), concubine of Sénapati Mataram, I 261, 262; II 108; III 3.

Adi Wijaya, sult. of Pajang (died 1587), see also Wijaya, I 61, 213, 216, 304, 308; II 22, 62, 85, 91; IX 21, 29, 30.

adu kemiri, game with kemiri nuts, III 101.

Adu Werna, residence of a man of religion (partisan of rd. Kajoran), VII 38, 42.

Aèng Mata, Aèr Mata, Ayer Mata, cemetery, Madura, I 172, 268; IV-1 31; IV-2 48.

Aernhem (Gerrit v.), lieut., V 236, 274.

Agĕng (ratu), queen-consort of Mangku Rat I, IV-2 1.

Agong, see Agung.

Agra Yuda (tg.), son of tg. Pasisingan (rebels against Mangku Rat I), IV-1 27, 28, 32.

Agra Yuda (capt.), Eur. deserter, Lesage, V 98, 183.

Agra Yuda (dem.), mantri under Truna Jaya, VI 280.

Agul-Agul (tg.), commander, V 79.

Agung (pg. or rd.), brother of Mangku Rat I, IV-1 1, 30.

Agung Badung (gusti), ruler in Bali, VIII 139, 152.

Agung (sult.), king of Banten, 1651-'82, VIII 27.

Agung (pan.), ruler of Giri, III 207; V 3, 13, 55; IX 76.

Agung Kajoran (pan.), pg. Maulana Mas, IV-2 40; VII 2/3, 8.

Agung (susuhunan), sunan Mangku Rat I, VIII 43.

Agung (sultan) of Mataram, 1613-'45, I 61, 69, 85, 89, 90, 102, 155, 164, 168, 177, 178, 184, 190, 191, 197, 198, 205, 219, 232, 233, 235, 237, 252, 260, 263, 271, 287-289, 292-294, 296, 300, 303, 309, 311, 313, 314; II 1, 3, 6, 12, 13, 41, 48, 59, 60, 88, 89, 115, 119, 123, 132; III passim; IV-1 1-7, 12, 13, 19, 23, 28, 35, 38, 53, 74, 86, 109; IV-2 1, 4, 14, 15, 28, 29, 31, 40, 42, 43, 48, 56, 57, 137; V 1-3, 4, 9, 21, 190; VII 4, 9; VIII 14, 63; IX 10, 16-19, 21, 35, 37-40, 43, 45-51, 54, 56-58, 66, 67, 70, 71.

Agus (pg.) of Kajoran, brother-in-law of Sénapati Mataram, I 311.

Ahmad Abdu'l-Arifin (sultan), of Demak, I 51, 73.

Ahmad-Muhammad, Jav. romance, I 255.

Ahmat (encik), Malay captain, IV-1 79, 80, 81, 94.

ajar, non-Islamic man of religion, I 186, 192, 247, 305.

Ajar (ng.), man of religion of mount Lawu, V 133; VII 48, 49.

Aji Pamasa, Jav. pseudo-history, I 306.

Aji Saka, mythical king, I 9, 273, 307, 318.

Ajuda palace in Lisbon (archives), I 260.

Akbar, Great Mogul of India, III 204.

Akkeren (van), author, I 311.

Akim, Mad. rebel, V 221.

Alad-alad (ng.), governor of Semarang, V 66; VIII 23, 127-130.

Alan, river, V 158.

Alap-alap (tg.), commanders under Sénapati, Krapyak and Agung, II 117, 118; III 28, 36, 41, 84, 93, 140, 209, 210.

al-Aqsā, mosque in Jerusalem, I 98.

cAlā'ad-Din Shah, king of Acheh, I 79, 273.

Albertsen (Hans), from Koningsbergen, soldier, V 201/2, 262.

Albuquerque (Afonso d'), vice-rey, I 44.

Alexander, king of Macedonia, see Baron Sakèndèr, Cariyosipun Sultan Iskandar, and Dhū'l-Ḳarnain.

"*Alfoeren*", natives of Ceram, soldiers, V 78.

Algarvia, South Portugal, I 76, 119.

Ali, Makasarese skipper, VIII 111.

'*Ali Ri'āyat Shah*, king of Acheh, I 273.

"*Alien*", village, V 107.

Alim (encik), interpreter, IV-2 163, 166; V 130, 202.

Alim (bagus), clerk, IV-2 138, 182.

Alit (pg.), brother of sunan Mangku Rat I, III 141, 251, 291; IV-1 1, 2, 15, 25, 27-33; IV-2 28, 46-48; VII 50; IX 55.

Alit (ratu), ratu Woh, daughter of sunan Mangku Rat II, V 113.

al-Kacbah, see Kaäba.

Al-Koran, holy scripture, IV-2 63; V 144, 189; VIII 121.

Al-Kuds, Al-Quds, Jerusalem, see Kudus, I 31, 97; II 130; IX 10.

Angga Suta, Mad. chief, V 162.

Angga Suta, guardsman of Mangku Rat I, IV-2 93.

Angga Wangsa, Jang Rana, governor of Surabaya, V 70, 201; VIII 51; IX 96.

Angga Wijaya, Madurese chief, IV-2 174.

Angga Yuda, rebel, son of pg. Tĕpa Sana, III 200; IV-2 15.

Angga Yuda, ambassador from Jambi, III 278.

Angga Yuda, brother of Angga Dipa of Sumĕnĕp, IV-2 59.

Angga Yuda, lurah, serving under pg. Alit, IV-1 29.

Angka Wiyu, annual religious ceremony and fair in Jati Nom, I 216, 309.

Angké, village west of Batavia, IV-1 104.

Angling Darma, legendary king, Jav. pseudo-history, I 126.

Angrok (kèn), Old Jav. ruler of Singasari, II 89.

Anjang Mas, ḍalang, wayang purwa, III 23.

Anjasmara, mountain, VI 290, 293, 309.

Anjou (Pieter d') from Lorcy, soldier, V 219, 262.

"*Ankesien*", village, V 275.

Annam, Annamites, Vietnamese, I 10, 23, 24, 271; IX 5.

Anom (pg.), bupati of Tuban, IV-1 195.

Anom (pg. ad.), name of sunan Mangku Rat II, IV-2 1; see Adipati.

Anom (raden adipati), son of pg. Madyun, V 249.

Anom (pan.), or arya Panular, Kajoran partisan, VII 8, 40, 46.

Anom (ratu), queen-consort of Mangku Rat I, mother of png. Puger, VII 9, 10.

Anom (sultan), of Cĕrbon, VIII 60, 85, 103; IX 97, 98.

Anom (kĕtib), theologian of Kudus, I 134.

"*Anongh-Anongh*" (ng.), commander, killed in battle, IV-2 125.

Ansaert (Marten) from Oostende, soldier, V 115.

Anta Dĕrsana (ng.), from Arosbaya, mantri, V 161.

Antaka Pura, cemetery of the Ratu Malang (died 1668), IV-1 14; IV-2 21.

Anta Kusuma, miraculous jacket, kyahi Gunḍil, I 30, 32, 94, 228; II 109.

Antang, mountain, see Ngantang.

Anyakra Kusuma, sultan Agung (name borne also by sunan Bonang), III 1, 26, 27, 129.

Anyakra Wati (Wadat), sunan Bonang, I 48; III 1.

Anyakra Wati, pan. Krapyak, III 1.

Appeldoorn, assistant, VIII 71, 73, 78, 90.

Aquilaria Malaccensis, "agelhout", kind of wood, III 73.

Arab, modality of Islamic worship in Lombok, I 100.

Arabia, Arabic, Arabs, I 11, 20, 22, 39, 48, 60, 122, 138, 140, 170, 251, 277, 282; II 99, 100; III 103, 266, 267, 269; IV-1 82; IV-2 94; IX 5.

Arakan, rice district, S.-E. Asia, IV-1 78, 96, 139.

Archaeological Commission, "Oudheidkundige Commissie", I 98, 99.

Archipelago (Indian), see also Indonesia, I 1, 5, 8-10, 13, 14, 17, 19, 24-26, 29, 51, 81, 98, 142, 148, 151, 170, 200, 203, 253, 255, 260, 299, 312, 317, 318; II 60, 84, 228; III 207; IV-1 69, 117; VIII 73, 133; IX 7, 29, 43, 59, 97.

"*Ardi Karun*", ĕmban, tutor to ki Wana Kusuma's sons, VII 46.

Ardi Menggala (ky.rd.), Madurese rebel, IV-2 144.

Ardi Wijaya, legendary king of Majapahit, I 131.

Arentsen (Joan), soldier, V 98.

Arga Dalem, Arga Déwa, legendary hermits of mount Merbabu, I 305.

Aris Baya, see Aros Baya.

Arja Balambangan, ruins of a kraton, III 256.

Armagon (Thomas), interpreter, IV-1 143.

Armentières, town (soldier), V 214, 219, 262.

Arnhem (town, museums), I 273; III 122; V 105.

Aros Baya, town, district, West Madura, I 69, 162, 169, 171-174, 176, 182, 215, 217, 288, 291, 294, 295, 314; III 38, 83, 84, 86-89, 92, 97, 137, 279; IV-2 55, 60, 68, 88, 174-178; V 161, 190; VIII 50; IX 16, 17, 50.

Aros Baya, Aris Baya (pg.ad.), ruler, III 92.

B

286, 287, 292, 304-306, 308-311, 313, 315, 316.

Babad Nitik, III 202.

Babad Pajajaran, II 74.

Babad Pasir, I 42, 56, 57, 251; II 74; III 118, 121.

Babad Sangkala, chronological table, I 15, 45, 53, 55, 57, 58, 129, 134, 146, 147, 249, 254, 255, 262, 266, 304, 309, 310, 312; II 4, 24, 30, 43, 54, 61, 62, 64, 65, 87, 89, 97, 111, 113, 114, 119, 123, 124, 129, 130; III 3, 11, 21, 22, 37, 46-48, 50, 92, 105, 108, 110, 111, 136, 167, 199, 211, 217, 222, 249, 261, 262, 277, 280, 289; IV-1 2, 11-13, 15, 27, 43, 53, 67, 141, 148; IV-2 3, 14, 16, 21, 22, 27, 29, 80; IX 4.

Babad (Sĕngkalaning) *Momana*, chronological table, I 87, 280; II 4, 12, 54, 64, 97, 111, 113, 114, 119, 123, 124, 129; III 3, 11, 22, 23, 25, 26, 29, 37, 48, 105, 110, 112, 212, 217, 222, 289; IV-1 11, 12, 14, 34, 36, 53, 67, 179; IV-2 3, 8, 9, 14, 16, 22, 26, 29.

Babad Songĕnĕp (Sumĕnĕp), chronicle, I 294; III 87; IV-2 59.

Babad Tawang Alun, I 298.

Babad Tuban, I 132, 136, 282, 283; III 49; IV-1 194.

"*Baba kaija Kiaffa*", lurah, IV-1 122.

Babarong, village, VIII 41, 63, 76, 78.

"*Babatack*", village, VI 288.

Bacingah (kuta), fortification, II 119, 121; IV-2 30.

Backer (Jacob), junior merchant, IV-1 85.

Baden, German town (soldier), V 215, 262.

Badoleng, rendez vous of Mataram forces, III 84.

badong, ornamental breastplate, II 122.

Badru'd-dīn (paté Rodin ?), ruler of Demak, I 46.

Badung, Den Pasar, town in Bali, I 208; VIII 152; IX 102.

Bagawanta, river, I 116; III 240; VII 26; IX 47.

Bagdad, Irak, Khalifate, I 29.

Bagdad (maulana), in holy war against Majapahit, I 54.

Bagĕlèn, district, south of Kĕdu, I 214, 225, 227, 302, 317; II 73, 102, 114;

III 120, 121, 139, 196; IV-1 17, 109; V 10, 23, 27, 62, 105, 125, 131, 138; VII 22-24, 26, 27, 32, 34, 42-44, 51; VIII 16, 39, 42, 65; IX 29, 32, 74, 76, 88, 89, 96.

"*Baginger*" (rd.), local chief, VII 7.

Bagna (ĕmpu), patih of West Madura, convert to Islam, I 171.

Bagus, Ambonese lieut., V 100, 137, 166, 167, 236; VI 292.

Bagus (encik), Malay captain, IV-1 98; IV-2 164, 165.

Bagus (rd.), name of Sénapati Mataram, II 22.

Bagus (rd.), rd. ad. Juminah, uncle of sult. Agung, II 111; III 2, 289.

Bagus Pati, Mad. commander, VII 26.

mBah Rawa, see Amba Rawa.

Bajul Sangara of Semanggi, legendary ancestor, I 208.

Bak (Jan), sergeant, V 98.

Baka (prabu, ratu), mythical king, I 220, 221, 310.

Baker (A.), British merchant in Banten, III 269, 270.

Bakker (Claes), junior surgeon, V 273.

Bal, capital of Campa, I 22.

Balabar (ky.), holy criss of Mataram, IV-2 193; VI 304.

Balawarti, locality near Kediri, see also Baluwarti, V 244.

balé, open hall, pavilion, II 125; III 106, 107, 115, 122.

Baléga, town in Madura, I 172, 173, 185; II 58; III 49, 84, 85, 89, 92, 93; IV-2 50; VI 294.

Baléga (pg.), Mad. commander, III 86.

balé kambang, artificial island with pavilion, I 140, 285.

Balé Kencur, hall surrounded by water in Tembayat, II 85.

Balé Lumur (ky.), holy coach of Majapahit, I 20.

Balé Panjang, river, V 154.

Bali, Balinese, I 1, 2, 5, 7, 8-12, 64, 80, 93, 131, 138, 141, 151, 156, 162, 166, 169, 177, 179, 182, 184, 187, 193-200, 208, 218, 221, 248, 255, 264, 265, 269, 288, 290, 296, 297, 299, 301, 305; II 37, 56, 60, 61, 67, 94; III 97, 132, 185, 203, 254, 255, 257-262, 284; IV-1 23, 25-27, 30, 32, 37, 39, 43, 50-52, 71, 79, 97, 102, 128, 160, 167;

Banyu Biru, village, I 257; II 17.

Banyu Dana, village, VIII 63, 85.

Banyumas, district, province, I 42, 56, 214, 254, 308; II 65, 74; III 120, 196; IV-2 189, 190, 192; V 38, 50, 63; VII 42; VIII 22, 32, 39, 41-43; IX 21, 29, 74, 76, 78, 88, 96.

Banyu Putih, village, VIII 67, 68, 70, 71.

Banyu Sumurup, cemetery near Ima Giri, III 88; IV-1 148; IV-2 8, 29.

Banyuwangi, town, district, (see Blambangan), I 64, 192, 193, 195, 255, 298, 300.

Bara Budur, Buddhist shrine, I 310.

Baran (encik), Malay, friend of kr. Galésong, IV-2 136.

Barat Tiga, tg. Singa Ranu, patih of sult. Agung, III 39.

Bareng, Wareng, village, IV-2 30.

Bari (Sèh), man of religion, I 25, 283.

Barong, capt. of cavalry, V 219.

Baron Sakèndèr, Jav. pseudo-history, legendary ancestor, see Alexander, I 245, 313; II 74, 88; III 157.

Baros, harbour, N. Sumatra, I 100, 268; IV-1 196.

Barreto de Resende (Pedro), historian, III 169.

Barros (João de), historian, I 44, 55, 251; II 67.

Baru (koja), Gujarat merchant, III 68.

Baru (ky.), holy lance of sult. Agung, III 140, 141; V 132; VII 49.

Baskara, Mad. prince, VIII 54, 57.

Bastinck (Willem), merchant, V 41, 44, 45, 57, 65, 69, 78, 128, 129, 143, 146, 174, 176, 188, 199, 201, 208, 213, 215-217, 231, 233, 236, 254, 256, 274.

Batang, district, III 247, 248; IV-1 1, 109, 126, 177; IX 54, 74.

Batang (ratu), sultan Agung's queen-consort, III 247.

Bata Putih, wall of the kraton Kuṭa Gedé, II 119.

Bata Putih, cemetery in Surabaya, V 201.

Batara Katong, ancestor of Panaraga regents, see also bhaṭāra, I 59.

Batara of Majapahit, divine king, I 22.

Batara Vigiaja (Wijaya), king of Dayo (Majapahit), I 52.

Batavia, capital (Jakarta), see also Castle and "Ommelanden", I 13, 31, 39, 71, 72, 107, 109, 116, 117, 125, 184, 194, 198, 205, 231, 238, 252, 257, 259, 284; II 103, 111; III 17, 55, 63, 66, 67, 69-76, 78-88, 90, 92, 94, 111, 112, 116, 117, 126, 127, 130-134, 137, 141, 144-153, 155-159, 162, 164-167, 169, 170, 172, 173, 176-179, 183, 184, 186-191, 193-195, 197, 199-201, 207, 217, 222-225, 229, 233-238, 241, 243, 245, 246, 251-253, 255, 256, 261, 262, 265, 266, 269, 270-272, 274, 275, 277, 281, 283-285, 287, 289; IV-1 passim; IV-2 4, 10, 12, 19, 22, 35-38, 65, 67, 70, 72-75, 78, 80, 81, 84, 95, 108, 111, 123, 124, 127, 130, 132-134, 139, 141, 146, 154, 155, 158, 160, 172, 180, 184, 193; V passim; VI 273, 281, 306; VII 17, 32; VIII 11, 19, 27-29, 33-35, 38, 43, 44, 47, 48, 53, 59, 72, 101, 103, 105, 107, 111, 131, 134, 136, 142, 148, 150, 151, 153, 154, 159, 161, 162; IX 12, 13, 20, 41-47, 49, 50, 53, 54, 56, 57, 59-63, 69-71, 76, 78, 80, 83, 88, 95-97, 99, 100-103.

Batavian Javanese, III 186, 245; V 35, 77, 79, 81, 98, 100, 101, 137, 166, 170, 179, 210, 218, 235, 236, 238, 241, 261, 265.

Batavian Malays, V 179, 210, 238/9.

Batavian Society of Arts and Sciences (K.B.G.), II 1, 3, 4, 64, 65; III 18, 225, 227, 279.

Batu, district, VI 274, 275, 277, 279, 280, 282, 283, 305, 308; IX 82.

Batu Benoang, Malay partisan of Surapati, VIII 134.

Batu Gilang, flat stone, seat, IV-2 80.

Batu Putih, see Bata Putih.

Batur, holy mountain, Bali, I 141.

Batu Rana, village, I 304.

Batu Rènggong, king of Bali, I 152, 195, 196, 288; II 61; IX 19.

Batu Tulis, Old Sundanese inscription, Bogor, I 117.

Bau Reksa (tg.) of Kendal, commander, III 59, 67, 69-71, 76, 81, 89, 106, 107, 119, 120, 127, 132-134, 144-146, 148, 153-158, 160, 179.

bawat, state sunshade, see lontar.

Bawean or Lubak, island, I 107, 136; II 125; III 18, 49; IV-1 59.

Baya Lali, town, see also Selimbi, V 28, 73.

Blitar, town, district, I 58, 164; II 101, 102; III 255; IV-1 189; V 64, 129, 248, 250, 252, 254; VI 274, 275, 285, 288, 289, 295, 301, 308; VII 48; IX 31, 82.

Blitar (pg.), png. Juminah, uncle of sult. Agung (see also Balitar), II 101-103; III 289; IV-1 5.

Blitar (pg.) II, son of pg. Blitar I, IV-2 15, 28, 115, 116, 118-122, 125, 140, 174; VII 15.

Blitar (ratu), wife of pg. Singa Sari, beloved of Mangku Rat II, IV-2 33, 34; V 61, 62, 157; VII 41; IX 67.

Blitar, Balitar (ratu mas), princess (18th cent.), III 213.

Blitung, see Billiton.

Blompot, ship, IV-2 81.

Blonck (Philip) from Rotterdam, drummer, V 214, 262.

Blora, town, district, I 58, 126, 129, 156, 162, 215, 221, 228, 270, 279, 281, 287; II 58, 107; IV-2 138, 182; V 25, 41, 42, 44, 77, 80, 88, 91, 102, 110, 112, 113, 114, 125, 128, 130, 133, 148, 150, 152, 153, 164, 170, 177, 188, 200, 264; VII 18, 21, 30; IX 32.

Bobat (paté), governor, see Bubat, I 157, 158.

Boboḍo, district (Pengging), see Bodo, I 209, 304.

Bocor, district (Bagelèn, Banyumas), I 57, 214, 254, 313; II 74; III 121; IV-2 188, 189.

Bocor (ki), mantri pamajĕgan under Pajang, I 308; II 74, 75; III 121; IX 30.

Bodleian Library, Oxford, I 304.

Boḍo (Jaka), legendary king (see Bobodo), I 208, 209, 304.

Boeij (Anth.), merchant, IV-1 54, 55, 57.

Bogaert (A.), clerk, II 126.

Bogor (Buitenzorg), I 109, 117, 118; IX 12.

Boisot (Adr.), Dutch prisoner of war, III 7.

Boja Nagara, town, district, I 126, 136, 215, 227, 279, 280, 304, 314; II 42, 48, 55; III 49.

"*Bokier*", river (= kali Widas ?), V 275.

Bokong (ny.ag.), sister of ki gedé Séséla, II 5, 6.

"*Bokor kumandang*" (Mendungan ?), village, V 119.

Bolton (W.), resident of Palembang, I 301; II 66.

Bommel, redoubt (Batavia), III 150.

Bonang, village, I 48, 133, 245.

"*Bonang* (book of)", Islamic theology, I 251, 283.

Bonang (sunan), preacher of Islam, I 48, 50, 51, 59, 92, 96, 101, 134, 140, 142, 145, 160, 245, 251, 283; II 29; III 1, 27, 129; VIII 19; IX 7.

Bonard (Carel) from Schouwen, soldier, V 98.

Boncong (kali), river, V 135.

Bondan Kejawan (rd., ky.), legendary son of Bra Wijaya, see also Arung Bonḍan, II 5-7, 48; see also Pondan.

Bone, Boni in South Celebes, kingdom (see Aru Palaka), IV-2 73, 75, 174; V 146, 189, 254; VI 276, 285.

Bongaai, Bungaya treaty, South Celebes, IV-2 62, 71, 72, 76; V 5, 6, 45, 189, 197, 208; VI 305.

Bongas, village, III 199.

Bonremedio, yacht, III 173.

Bonthain (kar.), son of Bonto Marannu, IV-2 62.

Bonto Marannu (kar.), Makasar chief, IV-2 62-70, 72, 74-76, 81, 82, 84-86, 88, 98, 110, 113; IX 68.

Borneo (Kalimanten), I 26, 43, 44, 46, 60, 152, 192, 254, 289; III 17, 18, 279, 280; IV-1 37, 63, 67, 68, 73, 87, 108; IV-2 75, 78, 88; V 29; IX 8, 15, 50, 56, 57.

Bosch (F. D. K.), orientalist, I 31, 270; II 10.

Botelho (Nuno Alvarez), admiral, III 164, 165, 230.

Both (Pieter), governor general, (1610-1614), II 129; III 20, 21, 24.

Boulenger (Jacques), historian, I 255.

"*Bouloubaulou*", haji (Makasar, Malay ?), IV-2 136.

Braband (Anthonij), ensign, V 98.

Braḍah (empu), legendary man of religion, see Bharada, I 296.

Brag (kali), river, V 135.

Brahim Asmara (makdum), father of png. Ampèl Dĕnta, I 20.

Brahmins, I 252; II 89.

Braja Pati, patih of Yuda Nagara, VIII 50, 54.

Bukit, see also Giri, III 207, 208.
Bukit (raja), sunan Giri, I 153, III 206, 207.
bulu bekti, tribute, I 214.
Bulan (orang kaya), Ambonese chief, IV-1 119.
Bulèlèng, town, district, Bali, IV-1 52; V 233, 252; VI 276; IX 56, 82.
Bulèlèng (Panji), Balinese commander, III 256, 257.
Bulèlèng Panaruka, Balinese soldier, V 98.
Bulon, village, V 269, 273.
Bumija, region of the Mataram kingdom, III 196.
Bundit (rd.ayu), wife of Nerang Kusuma, V 66.
Bungas (sèh), religious leader, III 199.
Bungaya, see Bongaai treaty.
Bunjala Driya (ki), partisan of Truna Jaya, VIII 41.
bupati, Jav. governor of a district, appointed by the king or the V.O.C., "regent".

Burèrèḥ (rd.), Abu Hurérah of Cempa, cousin of png. Ngampel, I 21.
"burgher", see "vrijburgher".
Bust (Joost v/d), from Brussels, soldier, V 165.
Busung Mernung, commander, IV-2 120.
Buta Ijo (tg.), commander, IV-2 100, 140; VII 15.
Buting (ki), son of tg. Mangku Yuda, V 68.
Buton, island, IV-2 62, 65, 71, 73.
Butuh, village, cemetery near Pajang, I 63, 99, 208, 210, 211, 217, 226, 255, 305, 306, 309; II 59, 87, 89, 91; III 37, 200, 212, 214; IX 30.
Butuh (ky. geḍé), teacher of Jaka Tingkir, II 17.
Buytenhem (Willem), assistant, IV-2 150, 151; see also Buijtenhem.
buyut, great-grandfather, I 257.
Buyut (ki) of Banyu Biru, legendary ancestor, II 17.
Buyut Dalem, cemetery near Boja Nagara, I 136; III 49.

C

Cabolang, Cĕntini, didactic poems, Jav. literature, III 219.
Cabolèk, village (Tuban), book, Jav. literature, I 134, 269, 283.
"Cabral", "Mardijker" lieut., V 236.
cacah, household (in census), II 46, 53, 118.
"Cacizes", Islamic clergymen (hajis ?), I 289.
Caeff (W.), Dutch resident in Banten, IV-2 67.
Caen (A.), lieut., III 70.
"Cahoenan" (rd.), brother of rd. Kajoran, IV-2 43; VII 7, 24, 25.
Cahyana (Banyumas), "Yayaha", village of Warsa Denti, VIII 41.

Cairo, Egypt, see also Mesir, I 254, 263, 266.
"Cajongam", district, town (Juwana ?), I 86-88, 144, 145, 262; IX 10.
cakal bakal, first settler, pioneer, II 8, 20.
Caket, river, II 39.
Cakra (rd.), pg. Selarong, IV-2 27.
Cakra Kusuma (prabu pandita), name of sult. Agung, III 26.
Cakra Nagara (pg.), prince of Sumĕnĕp, III 87.
Cakra Ningrat I, ruler of Sampang, I 172, 174, 293; III 86, 91; IV-1 31; IV-2 47-49, 59, 175; V 4.
Cakra Ningrat (II), ruler of Madura,

Cĕnṭini, encyclopedic poem, Jav. literature, I 4; III 219; see also Cabolang.

Ceporan, village, III 142.

Cĕrbon, town, kingdom (Ceribon, Cheribon), see also Gragè, I 7, 10, 22, 28, 37, 38, 41, 49-51, 56, 67, 69, 74, 77, 82, 86, 92, 94-97, 99, 105-107, 109-117, 119, 120, 123-125, 130, 131, 134, 141, 153-155, 227, 231, 240, 252, 260, 265, 275-278, 283, 291, 312, 314; II 14, 25, 27, 28, 47, 50, 53, 68, 114-116; III 14, 50, 58, 87, 88, 93, 94, 109, 110, 116, 128, 129, 131, 132, 150, 153, 166, 178, 185, 191, 195, 196, 220-222, 247, 248, 264, 273, 282, 283, 287; IV-1 1, 5, 18, 39-42, 51-53, 60, 104, 107, 141, 147; IV-2 2, 12, 23, 42, 88, 133-135, 148, 187; V 8, 11, 61, 92, 94, 146, 164; VII 7, 19, 22, 33; VIII 22, 27, 32, 35, 36, 38, 46, 47, 60, 63, 85, 103, 105, 109, 110, 127, 136, 155, 156; IX 7, 8, 11, 12, 15, 32, 44-46, 48, 50, 54, 56, 61, 66, 70, 73, 76, 87, 96-98.

Cerbon (pg.arya), Kasepuhan, author (?), I 275.

Cerbon (sunan), see Gunung Jati.

Cermé, village, V 148.

Cĕṭa, temple in Central Java, I 208, 209.

Ceṭa, village, V 127.

Ceylon, Sri Langka, I 31, 119; II 59; III 228; IV-1 159; IV-2 172; V 3, 54, 63; VIII 165; IX 103.

"*Chamda*", district (Saḍèng ?), I 187, 188, 194; IX 18.

Champa, see Cĕmpa.

Chanhoen, Chinese trader, IV-2 82.

Cheng Ho, Chin. admiral, IX 5.

Cheribon, see Cĕrbon.

"*Chily Poete*", Moslim Chinese, III 66, 270.

China, Chinese, I 1, 2, 5-7, 9-11, 13, 17, 27, 36-39, 60, 86, 97, 104, 106, 109-111, 113, 119, 130, 137, 138, 146, 154, 158, 159, 175, 200, 218, 239, 240, 249, 250, 258, 266, 270, 271, 274, 276, 284, 300, 308, 318; II 7, 95; III 16, 21, 62, 63, 66, 68, 91, 147-149, 151, 176, 180, 190, 199, 215, 216, 248, 254, 256, 280, 287; IV-1 20, 21, 51, 56, 57, 76, 79, 80, 82, 83, 88, 93, 97, 101, 107, 110, 113, 114, 116, 117, 137, 139, 151, 180, 183, 188,

199-203, 206, 208; IV-2 4, 54, 82, 89, 98, 123, 160; V 17, 19, 23, 54, 60, 96, 176, 204, 220, 221; VIII 26, 27, 29, 36, 60, 111, 112, 134, 155-158, 166; IX 5, 7, 11, 14, 15, 39, 42, 44, 46, 59, 61, 63, 77, 94, 100-102.

Christian, Christianity, I 76, 190, 195; II 56; III 205, 230, 231, 236; IV-1 83; IV-2 160; VI 291; VIII 73.

Christiaanse (Nicolaas), lieut., V 103.

Christiania (Oslo), town (soldier), V 165, 167.

chronicles, Jav. literature, see Babad, also Kronijk.

Ciasem, district, West Java, III 197.

Ci Atap, "Tsiattap", village, district, VII 47; VIII 15.

Cica Nala, medicine-man, V 113.

Cidurian, river, IV-2 66.

Ci Keruh, village near Sumedang, III 158.

Cilacap, seaport, III 239; VIII 154.

Cilincing, village, country-seat, IV-1 144.

Cili Pati (ki), envoy, IV-1 40.

Ci Liwong, river of Batavia, Jakarta, I 109, 117; III 133, 149, 152; IV-1 183.

Ci Manuk, river, West Java, I 109; III 195, 196.

Cina (aru), Makasar chief, V 270.

Cina (putri), queen-consort of Bra Wijaya, see China, II 7.

Cindaga, "Tsintagga" (kali), river, V 159.

Ciṇḍula, see Siṇḍula.

Ci Ompo, "Tsiompo", village, district, VII 47.

Ci Pontang, river, IV-2 66.

Cipta Naya, bupati of "Jatra" (Ceta ?), V 127, 168.

Cipta Raga, messenger, V 112, 168.

Cipta Raja, Javanese from Paṭi, V 116.

Cipta Wangsa (ky.lurah), envoy, IV-1 154.

Cirebon, see Cĕrbon.

Ci Sadané, river, V 17.

Ci Tanduwi, river, III 196.

Ci Tarum, river, I 42; IV-1 48, 93, 109, 111, 145; V 17.

Citra (lurah), horse expert, IV-1 122.

Citra Antaka (ky.lurah), envoy, IV-1 165.

Citra Menggala (ng.), messenger, V 105.

Citra Nala (si), tg. Paṭi's brother, IV-1 88, 92, 94, 109.

Couto (Diego de), Port. historian, I 79, 80, 82, 273; II 33, 34, 58, 67, 68, 85, 126.

Cowan (H. K. J.), orientalist, I 22.

Coylan, town (Malabar), V 6.

Craan (Pieter), lieut., V 78, 97-99, 101, 202.

Cranganor, town (Malabar), V 6.

Crape (Roel.), Danish trader, III 233.

Crawfurd (J.), British author, II 84.

criss, kris, creese, I 70, 95, 144, 247, 248; II 31, 34, 74; III 100, 125.

crocodiles, see Sangara.

Croes (Jacob), skipper, IV-1 194.

Croes (Manuel), Portuguese captain, IV-1 54.

Crucq, (K. C.), orientalist, I 76, 119, 260; III 56, 130, 227, 267; IV-2 90, 91.

"Cu-Cu", ruler of Demak, I 36, 38, 40, 41, 45, 46, 109, 110; II 7.

Cucu Angga Suta, "Tsoesoe Angazoeta" (ng.), Mad. rebel, V 162, 221.

"Cucuf" (paté), ruler of Gresik, I 139, 142, 143, 284.

Culi (kyai), criss of Mandaraka, II 127.

Cunaeus (J.), ambassador, V 5.

"Cun-Cĕh", ruler of Demak, I 36, 38.

cungkub, sepulchral dome, I 151.

Curing, village, V 46, 218, 225, 227, 228, 231, 232.

"Curuda", rebel from Bagelèn, VIII 39.

D

Dabul (Dabhol), port in Malabar, III 268.

Dadapan (rangga), companion of pan. Rama, VII 35.

Ḍaḍa(p) Pĕṭak, (residence of) legendary man of religion on mount Brama, I 245.

Daḍap Tulis (arya), Anḍap Tulis, son-in-law of ky. Pamanahan, II 50.

Dadap Tulis (tg.carik), secretary, I 280.

Ḍaḍung (kali), river, V 134.

Daeng, Makasar title, VIII 39.

"Dagertije" (tg.), Yuda Karti (?), commander, III 261.

Dagol, district (Keḍung Dawa), V 118.

Daha, Kaḍiri, town, kingdom, I 55, 253; II 62.

Daka Wana, messenger, IV-1 29.

ḍalang, performer, wayang theatre, I 258.

dalem, mansion, II 53.

Dalem (Kuṭa), Kuṭa Gĕḍé, II 120, 121.

Dalem (ky.), husband of ratu Malang, IV-2 15-17.

Dalem (pg.), ruler of Tuban, I 135, 136; III 49.

Dalem (sunan), ruler of Giri, I 143-148; II 60; IX 15.

Dalĕm di Madé, king of Gèlgèl, Bali, I 300.

Dalit (Entol), inferior official, Banten, I 302.

Dam (Jan v.), lieut., V 115, 126, 137, 165-167.

Dam (Johan v.), governor of Ambon, V 52.

Damar (arya) of Palembang, legendary ancestor, I 38, 106, 200, 202, 300, 301; II 7.

Damar (rd.mas), pg.ad. Purbaya, III 2; IV-1 6.

Damar Wulan, legendary hero (Majapahit), I 185, 186, 192.

Damar Wulan, pseudo-history, Jav. literature, I 52, 166, 186, 192, 246, 282, 292, 295, 297, 298; III 213.

Dampak, village, V 87.

ḍampar kencana, golden throne, III 26, 129.

Dana Laya, pleasure garden, Mataram, III 22.

E

F

Faber (G. H. von), author, III 14, 47.
Fadhillah Khan, Falatehan (?), sunan Gunung Jati, I 277.
Fakhru'llah, Tagaril, sunan Gunung Jati, I 276.
faķīh, Islamic lawyer, I 67, 292.
Fakīh Nağmu'd-Dīn, Banten, high judge, I 279.
fakir, man of religion, VI 300.
Falatehan, sunan Gunung Jati, I 50, 112, 252, 276, 277; IX 11.
Fath, victory (Falatehan), I 276.
Fātimah bint Maimūn, Putri Lèran, gravestone, I 21.
Fattāḥ, victor (Patah), I 35; IX 7.
Fennema (R.), geologist, V 135, 140, 143, 144.
Fernandus (Diego), "Mardijker" lieut., III 241.
Ferrari, (P. Bernardino), R. C. missionary, I 190.
Ferry Charter, Majapahit, I 157, 257, 279, 280, 284, 290, 304.
Filet (P. W.), author, II 11.
fiqh, Islamic religious law, I 67, 258.
Flamang, ship, V 257.
Flanders, Vlaanderen, province (soldier), V 262.

Flemings, Dutchmen (in English reports), III 62, 65.
Flines (E. W. v. Orsoy de), collector of China, II 18.
Foreest (jhr. H. A. van), Linschoten Vereeniging, V 141.
Formosa, Taiwan, island, V 55.
Fortuyn, ship, V 188, 256.
France, French, IV-1 198; IV-2 54; V 13, 31, 226; VIII 59, 100, 155.
Francen (Corn.), Bandanese burgher, IV-2 54.
Francen (J.), lieut., VIII 151.
Franciscan friars, I 298, 299.
Franken (Jan), from Nijmegen, soldier, V 215, 262.
Franssen (Pieter), ambassador, III 99, 163, 174-177, 198, 200, 201, 281.
Franszen Holsteyn, see Holsteyn (Jan Franszen).
French, see France.
Friday service in the mosque, III 103, 114, 122, 203.
Friedericy (H. J.), author, V 134.
Fruin-Mees (Wilha), historian, III 95, 163, 178, 185.
Further India, "Achter-Indië", see also India, I 1, 7, 10, 22, 238, 239; IV-1 87.

G

Gabang, see Gĕbang.
Gabus, village, V 86.
Gaḍing, pleasure garden south of the kraton, III 23, 111, 112, 290.
Gadongan, mountain, VI 292, 308, 309.
Gagak Baning (pg.), ruler of Pajang,

prince of Mataram (rd. Tompé), I 219; II 99, 100.
Gagak Pranala (pg.), ruler of Pajang (Gagak Baning), II 100.
Gagak Rimang, horse of arya Panangsang, II 39, 41.

Gĕṇḍing, district, I 84, 188, 189, 194, 230, 297, 315; IX 18.
Gĕṇḍing (dipati), bupati, II 122; III 4, 5, 8.
Geni Rongga, lurah in Panaraga, III 9.
Gent (Hendr. v.), resident of Jambi, III 278; IV-1 85, 94, 96, 97.
Gĕṇṭayu, mythical king, I 156, 290.
Gerber (Joan), soldier, V 121.
Gerbertsen (Pieter) from Hannover, soldier, V 121.
Gericke (J. F. C.), Roorda (Taco), javanists, III 9; IV-2 48.
Gerih, village, V 137, 140.
Gerongan, port in East Java, IV-2 81, 87.
Gesik, district of Tuban, IV-1 195.
Getas, village in Grobogan, II 7.
Getas Pandawa (ki.), legendary ancestor, II 5-7.
Gijsels (Artus), governor of Ambon, III 13, 14, 16, 56, 59, 62, 69, 78, 206, 207, 265, 281.
Gili Maṇḍangin, island, see Mandangin.
Giri, town, holy community, state, I 12, 21, 21, 28, 60, 77, 83, 92, 95, 100, 101, 106, 115, 137-155, 163, 167, 168, 174, 182, 183, 190, 196, 197, 215, 219, 245, 252, 265, 268, 284-292, 295, 308, 314, 315; II 24, 37, 58, 60-64, 95, 98, 102, 104-106; III 7, 8, 29, 36, 37, 47, 50, 86, 88, 93, 132, 152, 197, 205-209, 213-220, 273; IV-1 157; IV-2 6, 7, 10, 13, 48, 64, 87, 94, 111; V 3, 6, 13, 45, 49, 55, 59, 69, 72, 81, 129, 143, 169, 173, 192-194, 196, 233, 249, 268, 275; VI 306; VII 49; IX 12, 14, 15, 21, 27, 29, 31, 40, 45, 46, 69, 76, 90, 91, 94.
Giri (sunan, pan., raja), spiritual ruler, I 26, 54, 60, 71, 115, 145, 153, 160, 170, 252, 260, 261, 268, 285, 287, 288, 292; II 37, 45, 52, 53, 60-63, 104, 105, 107, 124; III 215, 219; IV-1 22; IV-2 48, 58, 94, 95, 111, 164; V 81, 150, 192, 194, 232; VII 50; IX 15.
Giri (pg.mas ing), ruler, IV-2 6, 13, 83, 111.
Giri Daya, West Borneo, I 289.
Giri Gajah Kaḍaton (sunan), author, I 285.
Giri Kusuma, ruler of Sukadana, Borneo, I 152.

Giri Laya, cemetery (Mataram), III 289, 290; IV-2 1.
Giri Laya (pan.), ruler of Cerbon, I 116; IV-1 39, 148; VII 19, 22; IX 56, 87.
Giring, district, I 222, 232, 234, 311, 313; II 51, 52; IV-1 6; IX 22, 28, 90.
Giring (ki geḍé), local chief, I 222; II 51, 52; IV-2 40; VII 3, 39, 40.
Giring (ky.) III, local chief, great-grandfather of Paku Buwana I, IV-2 44.
Giri Pura, Giri, III 47.
Gissing (kali), river, V 131.
Glotok (kali), river, V 154.
Goa, capital of Port. India, III 1, 20, 165, 166, 168-172, 177, 223-229, 231, 284; IX 43, 44, 46.
Goa, archbishop of, I 76.
Godon (Jan), from Nieuwpoort, soldier, V 165.
Godong (Gogodong), village, I 35, 259; V 30, 37, 39, 41, 42, 77, 80, 83, 86, 87, 97, 101, 117, 122, 212; VII 30.
"*Goemenol*", Gumĕna, village (Gresik), I 286.
Goens (Rijcklof v.), ambassador, governor general, 1678-1681, II 47, 77, 116; III 1, 9, 23, 51, 90, 91, 104, 106, 108, 110, 113, 116, 121, 123, 128, 129, 133, 142, 143, 162, 163, 167, 168, 212, 233, 234, 236-238, 241, 247-249, 251, 253, 267, 271, 272, 285, 286, 290, 291; IV-1 v, vi, 1-7, 10, 11, 15-17, 19, 23, 25, 27, 30-36, 39, 40, 42, 43, 53, 68, 74, 76, 78-81, 85-91, 93-98, 100, 110, 111, 119, 127, 129, 171, 205; IV-2 1, 2, 27-19, 79, 95, 142, 146, 153, 154; V 3, 5, 34, 65, 93, 96, 196, 266; VII 7, 9, 50; IX 48, 54, 55, 58, 59, 62.
"*Gogok*" (rd.), grandson of pg. Tepa Sana, IV-2 142.
Goijer (Pieter de), ambassador, IV-1 56.
Golconda, kingdom in India, IV-1 139.
Gombong, seaport (Pasuruhan), IV-2 70, 87, 88, 100, 136; VI 275.
Goossens (J.), senior merchant, IV-1 85.
"*Goude*" (rd.), son of sunan Mangku Rat I, IV-2 192; VII 23.
Goudvink, ship, V 189.
Goutappel, ship, V 78.
"*Goutsie*", Chinese correspondent, V 151, 176.

II 51, 82-84, 93, 94; IV-1 179; VII 21, 31, 35, 37, 39-42, 43-46; VIII 14, 16; IX 22, 88-90.

Gunung Prahu, mountain, Central Java, III 43.

Gunung Sari, quarter of the town of Kaḍiri, V 227, 244, 245.

Gunung Sembung, Gunung Jati (Cĕrbon), I 114, 276.

Gunung Wujil, Wijil, grave of png. Silarong, IV-2 30.

Gurana (daëng), Makasar chief, V 273.

Gusté Paté, Gusti Patih, grand-vizier of Majapahit, I 35, 52, 87, 127, 142, 144-146, 158, 159, 170, 180, 181, 188, 194, 253, 295; IX 8.

Gusti Panji Sakti, of Bulèlèng, Bali, I 264.

Guwa Babar, fortification, Tuban, I 135; III 49.

Guwa Langsé, cave, residence of Ratu Lara Kidul, II 76, 83, 84; III 288.

H

Haan (F. de), archivist, II 115, 120; III 92, 195, 196 IV-1 190; IV-2 63.

Haan (H. de), surgeon, author, II 88, 119, 120; III 25, 27, 50, 59, 72-74, 80-82, 99, 100, 107, 112-114, 117, 118, 120, 123, 124, 136, 138, 283; V 56; VIII 28, 59.

Hagedoorn (Hendr.), sergeant, V 98.

Hageman (J.), historian, I 55, 149; II 4, 54, 57-59, 61-64, 66, 89, 90, 92, 97-100, 114, 123, 129; III 6, 11, 27, 47, 83, 95, 206, 219; IV-1 147.

Hagen (Lambert Dirckxz), senior merchant, III 24.

Haghen (Steven v/d), admiral, III 15, 19.

Hainault (Henegouwen), soldier, V 262.

haji, pilgrim to Mecca, I 118, 269, 289; VIII 119.

Haji (ky.), "Moorish priest", sult. Agung's envoy, III 158, 252, 269-272; IV-1 75.

Haji, sultan of Banten, V 61.

Hall (D. G. E.), historian, I 247.

Hamza Pansuri, Sumatran theologian, I 100, 268.

Hannover, town (soldier), V 121.

Hanoman, monkey king, wayang, IV-2 172.

Hansen (Jan), from Christiania, ensign, V 165, 167.

Hansen (Pieter), from Amsterdam, sailor, V 118.

Happel (Joh. Maur. v.), lieut., VIII 128.

Harde (Jan de), merchant, IV-1 169, 170, 173; V 20, 80, 129, 143, 169, 182, 188, 194, 196, 197, 208, 233, 249, 256-258, 271-273.

Harmagon (Thomas), interpreter, IV-2 11.

Harmensz. (Gerrit), corporal, V 165.

Harren (Harm. v.), skipper, IV-2 178.

Hartingh (Nic.), author, IV-1 8.

Hartman (Andries), lieut., V 78, 98-100, 137, 165-167.

Hartogh (Joh. de), resident of Japara, VIII 25, 28, 35, 42, 45, 58, 106, 111-113, 115, 116, 128.

Hartsinck (Willem), captain, IV-2 173.

Haruku, island, I 289.

Harunarrasjid Tuammenanga-rilampana (karaeng), ruler of Tallo', South Celebes, IV-2 71, 75.

Hasanuddin, king of Banten, I 56, 73, 74, 105, 106, 114, 115, 120-122, 204; II 35; IX 12; see Hikayat.

Hasanuddin Tuammenanga-riballa'-pangkana, ruler of Gowa, South Celebes, IV-2 71; V 5, 6, 189.

Hasenberg, ship, V 188, 190.

Hative, village in Ambon, I 106, II 37.

Hayam Wuruk, Ayam Wuruk, king of

I 68, 98, 247, 251, 254, 259, 270, 281, 293; II 12; IV-2 182; V passim; VII 30, 31, 48, 49; VIII 11, 59, 149; IX 78-82.

Hurdt ("juffrouw"), Hurdt's wife, V 48.

Hurt (M.), junior merchant, IV-1 61.

Husain (lĕbé), governor of Cĕrbon, I 38.

Husain, grandson of Muhammad, ancestor of sunan Gunung Jati, I 291.

Hyang plateau, Eastern Corner of Java, I 193.

I

Ibn Molana (sèh), sunan Gunung Jati, I 22, 112; III 110.

Ibrahim, png. Atas Angin, of Karang Kamuning, I 48.

Ibrahim (koja), envoy from Makasar, IV-1 69, 72, 120, 121.

Ibrahim Asmara (maulana), legendary ancestor, I 20.

Ibu (ratu), queen-consort of sult. Agung, IV-1 34, 36.

Ibu (ratu), wife of Cakra Ningrat I, IV-1 31; IV-2 48.

Ibu Kali Tuwa (mahadum), nyahi geḍé Moloko (?), I 153.

Ijèn mountains, Eastern Corner of Java, I 64.

ilmu gaib, occult science, III 202.

Imagiri, cemetery of Mataram rulers, I 172; II 120; III 88, 110, 162, 247, 283, 289-291; IV-1 29; IV-2 8, 47, 48, 186, 188, 189, 191, 192; V 2, 10; VII 9, 23; VIII 19; IX 51.

Imagiri (pg.), pg. Cakra Ningrat I, IV-2 47.

imam of the mosque of Demak, I 47-50; IX 7, 8.

Ima Reksa, son of Wangsa Dipa, IV-1 193; IV-2 130.

"*Imbassadana*", Chinese harbour master, Japara, IV-1 21, 175, 196, 199-201, 204.

Imhoff (G. W. baron van), governor general, 1743-'50, I 268; III 157.

"*Indabangh*" (ng.), son of Wangsa Dipa, IV-2 124.

India, "Voor-Indië", Hindustan, Indian, see also Further India, I 1, 2, 9, 10, 11, 13, 25, 48, 220, 221, 260, 299; III 19, 50, 98, 165, 168, 169, 207, 226, 233, 318; IV-1 97, 117, 139, 140; V 54; VIII 59; IX 5, 60, 73, 77, 100.

Indian Ocean, see Southern Ocean.

Indo China, see also Annam, Cempa, I 10, 271; IX 5.

"*Indo-Chinese*", half-breed, peranakan, descendants of Indo-Chinese and Indonesians in Java, I 6, 24, 26, 109, 218, 318; II 95; IX 3.

Indonesia, "Oost-Indië", Indonesian, see also Archipelago, I 2, 3, 7, 8, 11, 13, 29, 71, 124, 245, 267, 282, 289, 297, 302; II 13, 69; III 55, 114, 131, 151, 248, 282; IV-1 58, 68, 95; IV-2 39; VI 291; IX 2, 41, 44, 71-73, 77-79.

Indra, Indian god, II 10; III 50.

Indra Bĕrma, prince of Campa, I 23.

Indragiri, kingdom, Sumatra, II 67, 68; IV-1 65.

Indra Jala, ship of dip. Tuban, III 50.

Indramayu, town, district West Java, I 109; III 199; IV-1 109, 111; IV-2 134; V 138, 257.

Indra Nata (tg.), Mataram, see Endra Nata.

Indrapura, Sumatra, I 205.

Ingalaga (pg.), Sénapati, II 101.

Ingalaga (pg., pan., raja, sunan), sult. Agung, III 27, 71, 72, 75, 99, 127, 128, 174, 268, 283.

Ingalaga Mataram (susuhunan), sunan Mangku Rat I, III 291; IV-1 3, 8; IX 54.

J

Jerawan, village, V 147.
Jeremiasz (Jan), prisoner of war, III 100, 235, 244.
Jeruk Lĕgi, village, V 272.
Jerusalem, holy city, al-Quds, I 31, 97, 98, 263, 268; II 130; IX 10.
Jesuit fathers, I 190, 289.
Jetis, village, V 270.
Jetmika (rd.mas), name of sult. Agung, III 27.
Jeumpa, port in Acheh, I 22, 245; IX 5.
Jibus, name of sunan Mangku Rat I, IV-1 1.
jim, Arab. jinn, spirit, II 82.
Jimantara (ky.), ruler in Sampang, IV-2 58.
jimat, amulet, III 139, 140.
Jimat (ki), holy cannon of Bantĕn, I 119.
Jimawal, 3rd year of windu, II 90.
Jimbun, locality, I 41.
Jimbun (sénapati, pan.), sultan of Dĕmak, I 250.
Jipang (Panolan), kingdom, I 73, 77, 79, 82, 83, 89, 96, 99, 101, 104, 126-129, 135, 136, 148, 161, 162, 202, 204, 212, 215, 218, 224, 272, 279-281, 287, 302, 303, 307, 310, 312, 314; II 13, 24, 26, 28, 31, 32, 38-40, 42-44, 48, 53, 55, 58, 91-94, 114, 131; III 49; IV-1 18; IV-2 138, 142, 182; V 25, 40-44, 69, 71, 72, 77, 80, 91, 97, 102, 107, 108, 112, 113, 125, 128, 130, 133, 136, 137, 141, 145, 148, 150-153, 156, 163, 164, 189, 250, 256, 264; VII 18, 21, 25, 30, 33; IX 9, 13, 20, 21, 26-30, 78.
Jiwa (lurah), envoy, IV-1 124.
Jiwa, petinggi, V 151.
Jiwa Raga (ky.), courtier, executed (sult. Agung), III 159, 253.
Jiwa Raga (ng.), Setia Yuda, courtier (Mangku Rat II), VIII 43, 91, 110, 123, 124, 145.
Jiwa Sraya, envoy from Cĕrbon, IV-1 41.
Jlantik, Balinese family, I 197, 299, 300; III 259.
Johan, Balinese soldier, V 165.
"*Joharsih*", Jorge d'Acunha, Port. ambassador, III 167, 168.
Johns (A.), orientalist, I 29, 247.
Johor, town, kingdom, I 22, 81, 105, 273; II 33; III 70, 82, 164; IV-1 54, 65, 67; VIII 73.

Jolang (rd.mas), name of pan. Séda-ing-Krapyak, I 233, 316; II 128; III 1; IX 33.
Jonassen (Evan), junior merchant, V 120, 162.
Jonathan, ship, IV-1 70.
Jonge (J. K. J. de), historian, archivist, II 119-121; III 7, 92, 95, 103, 145, 158, 159, 252; IV-2 39; VI 273, 280; VII 5, 6, 12, 18, 35, 48; VIII 104.
Jongh (Max. de), ambassador, IV-1 161, 181, 183-187, 190, 199.
Jonker (capt.), Ambon. commander, V 10, 78; VI 273, 282, 286-301, 306; VIII 11, 106, 107, 153; IX 83.
Jortan, quarter of Gresik, III 16, 17, 21, 53, 64, 68, 71, 81, 82, 90, 205-207; IV-2 88; IX 40; see also Jaratan.
"*Jouw Soeta*", of Gresik, servant, IV-2 97.
Juan Pedro Italiano, Venetian renegade (pan. Krapyak), III 24, 25.
Judah (Molana), man of religion, Bantĕn, see also Jedda, I 122.
Jugul Muḍa, Jav. law code, I 129.
Juldah, country of Wali Lanang, I 140.
Julig (rd.mas), son of Sénapati Mataram, II 111.
Jumadil-akbar (sèh), legendary holy man of Islam, I 38.
Jumadil-akir, 6th month of Jav. year, IV-2 111.
Jumadil-awal, 5th month of Jav. year, IV-2 191.
Jumadi'l-Kubrā (shaikh), legendary holy man of Islam, I 20, 245, 248, 250, 268.
Jumahat, Friday, III 114.
Jumilah (rd.ayu), consort of Sénapati Mataram, II 111.
Juminah, district, Blitar, II 101.
Juminah (pg.ad.), son of Sénapati Mataram, II 101, 103, 111, 112; III 2, 44, 45, 118, 158, 160, 161, 289; IX 31.
Junghuhn (Fr. W.), geologist, I 31; V 133, 135, 148, 149.
Jung Mara, Japara, port, I 104, 269, 270.
Jurang Jero, river, V 154.
Jurang Jero, village, III 85, 86, 93.
Jurang Parahu or *Palwa*, village, III 43.
Jurle (Steven), from Lausanne, soldier, V 165, 167.

K

Kerta, see Karta.

Kerta Jaya, commander, IV-2 127.

Kerta Nagara, Old Jav. king of Singasari, I 199.

Kerta Sana, town, district, I 164; II 118; IV-2 141, 142; V 41, 43, 44, 71, 72, 113, 130, 141, 142, 145, 151, 152, 156, 163, 164, 168-170, 172-175, 180, 181, 183, 185, 187, 193, 194, 252, 268, 269, 274, 275; VI 276; IX 80, 82.

Kerta Sana (arya), bupati, V 72, 91, 97, 187, 193, 194, 198, 211, 230, 231, 250.

Kĕrtopapatti, Old Jav. judge, I 66.

Kĕṭa, Old Jav. shrine, mount Lawu, I 187, 297, 310.

Ketangga, river, V 132, 139.

Ketawangan, Katawĕngan (ng.), ruler of Kaḍiri, III 31, 84, 93, 94, 97; V 31, 249, 254.

kĕtib anom, mosque official, see also katib, I 269.

Kĕtib ing Giri, author, III 213.

Keulen (Cologne), town (soldier), V 51, 105.

Keurbeek, ensign, VIII 84.

Kéyan Santang, Sundanese mythical ancestress, I 277.

Kéyong Uwi, river, area, V 108, 110, 111, 113, 114, 150.

Keyser (Pieter Dircksz.), navigator, II 98.

Keyts (Joh.), bookkeeper, IV-1 161.

Khalif, Khalifate, I 29, 51, 70.

Kiauko, Chinese harbour-master, VIII 129, 156.

Ki Dang Palih (kyahi), ruler(s) of Grĕsik, I 146, 147.

Kidul (Gunung), Southern Hills, II 52.

Kidul (nyahi lara), goddess of the Southern Ocean, II 76, 79, 82, 83; see Lara.

Kidul Ngardi, district of Tuban, IV-1 195.

Kidung Pamancangah, Balinese chronicle, I 198, 297; II 60; III 259.

Kidung Sunda, Old Javanese poem, I 117, 275; IX 11.

Kieft (Winrick), ambassador, IV-1 11, 36, 98, 101-103, 106-108.

Kilèn (ratu), Kulon, princess of Kajoran, IV-2 41.

"*Kinang*" (gunung), mountain, VII 43.

Kinitrèn (rd. mas), son of Sénapati Mataram, see Kanitrèn, I 296; II 111.

Kiping, village, V 121, 132-134.

Kirtya Liefrinck-van der Tuuk, library in Singaraja, Bali, I 269, 299.

Kisik, Kikisik, village in Madura, III 86.

Klagèn, village, river, V 137, 145.

klangĕnan, amusement. Juru Taman, II 88.

Klaṭèn, town, district, I 61, 62, 145, 211, 216, 230, 234; II 13; III 93; IV-2 43; VII 8, 9, 38; VIII 4, 253; IX 67, 86.

Klepu, village, V 111.

Kleting Biru (rd. ayu), princess, sister of Mangku Rat II, V 240.

Kleting Ijo (rd. ayu), princess, VII 6.

Kleting Kuning (rd. ayu), sister of Mangku Rat II, V 240; VII 23.

Kleting Wungu (rd. ayu), sister of Mangku Rat II, V 240; VI 273.

Kling, man of Coromandel, IV-1 196.

Klinkert (H. C.), orientalist, I 38.

Klitrèn, quarter of Yogyakarta, I 296.

Klotok, mountains in Kaḍiri, V 157, 203.

Klumpang, village, East Java, V 45, 192, 275.

Klungkung, capital, Bali, I 93, 264; IX 17.

Kluwang, village, V 108, 111; VII 48.

Knebel (J.), author, I 98, 251, 259, 266; III 121.

Knol (Govert), commander, IX 103.

kobongan, central room of Jav. house, with shrine, see also patanèn, I 31; II 10.

Koci, Kuci, kingdom, at war with Cĕmpa, I 22, 23 (Cochin China).

Kock (A. H. W. de), author (Palembang), I 301, 302.

Koda Panolé Songenep, legendary ancestor, see Kuda Panolih.

Kodrat (encik), Gujarat.

Kodrat (encik), envoy, IV-1 76.

Koentjaraningrat, author, I 303.

Koja (sèh), sèh Manganti, uncle of sunan Dalem of Giri, I 146.

Kombara, island (Palembang), IV-1 55.

Konang Pasir, Madurese commander, VIII 81.

Koningsbergen, town (soldier), V 202, 262.

Ko-Po (Cèk-), from Munggul, ancestor of the Demak family, I 36, 38, 41, 46.

Koripan, kingdom, see Kahuripan.

Kulon (ratu), daughter of pg. Pekik, of Surabaya, mother of Mangku Rat II, III 249.

kuluk, fez, I 259; II 25; III 100, 104.

Kumambang (mas), metre, Jav. macapat verse, I 268.

Kumambang (ratu), legendary queen of Japan (Majapahit), I 176.

Kumar (mrs. Ann), authoress, I 94.

Kumara, legendary king of Majapahit, I 283.

Kumba Karna, fortification of Tuban, I 283; III 49.

Kumba Rawa, Kumba Rawi, cannon in Japara, IV-2 91, 130.

Kung (aru), Makasar chief, V 270.

Kuning (sunan), mas Garendi, pretender (Kartasura), II 59.

Kuning (rd. mas), name of sunan Mangku Rat II, IV-1 12; IV-2 1.

Kunst (J.), musicologist, II 79.

Ḳur'ān, see Al-Koran.

Ḳuripan, see Kahuripan.

Kusèn, pěcat taṇḍa of Terung, I 200, 290.

Kusuma Brata, envoy, V 128.

Kuṭa Bacingah, fortification of Sěnapati Mataram, I 312; see also Kota.

Kuṭa Dalem, kuṭa Geḍé, residence of Sénapati Mataram, II 120, 121.

Kuṭa Geḍé, kraton, Kuṭa Dalěm, residence of Sénapati Mataram, I 224, 232, 312; II 6, 21, 25, 90, 120, 121; III 22, 23, 25, 104, 113, 115, 288; IV-2 80, 191; V 2; IX 38, 51.

Kutai, kingdom, Borneo, I 152, 289.

Kuṭa Jaba, Yogyakarta, I 121.

Kuṭa Rěnon, Lumajang, III 28, 30.

Kuwel, village, IV-2 29.

L

Labetaka, island in the Banda archipelago, III 18.

labuh, religious offerings, Jav. custom, I 311.

Lakiu, kingdom, connected with Campa, I 22.

Lacotier (Thom.), prisoner of war, III 101.

Laen (J. v/d), commander, IV-1 58.

Laeren, ship, IV-2 123.

Lagawa, rebel, VII 44.

"*Lagonder*", village, see also Lo Gěndèr, Salimbi, V 76, 89; VIII 33.

Lajer, village, V 111.

Lajěr, man of religion, envoy, V 213.

Laksamana (demang), patih of Japara, admiral, I 107, 123, 273; II 34, 36, 126; III 51, 119, 136, 165, 179-182, 188, 228; IV-1 82; V 146, 217, 247, 262; VIII 26, 116.

Lambert, prisoner of war, III 233.

"*Lamona*" (tg.), envoy, V 102, 104.

Lamongan, town, district, I 58, 146, 147, 164; III 12, 22.

Lampong, province, South Sumatra, I 120, 121, 204, 205, 279, 281, 303; III 275; IV-1 40, 49; VIII 44.

Lanang (kali), river, II 31.

Lanang (wali), legendary man of religion, Arab, father of sunan Giri, I 140, 141.

Lanang Dangiran, ky. Brondong, father of Jang Rana, V 201.

Landak, district, Borneo, III 17, 81; IV-1 144.

Landman, ship, V 272.

"*Landsarchief*", Batavia, Archives, Arsip Negara, Jakarta, II 1.

Langis Pati, commander, IV-2 182.

Langka, Sri Langka, see Ceylon.

M

Madyun (pg.), under Mangku Rat II, V 249.

Madyun (tg.), commander under pan. Juminah, III 161.

Madyun (tg.), name of ng. Wira Dikara, IV-1 189.

Maen (Gijsbert v/d), merchant, IV-1 97.

Maetsuycker (Joan), governor general (1653-'78), IV-1 21, 116, 135; V 34, 94.

Maetsuycker (Wilhem), junior merchant, IV-1 97.

Magdalena, wife of M. Pietersen, IV-1 87.

Magelang, town, IV-2 145.

Magelhaens (F. de), navigator, I 45.

Magĕtan, Kamagetan, town, district, I 229, 296; IV-2 138, 182; V 126, 142, 144; VII 18.

Mahmud (encik), ambassador, IV-1 69.

Mahmud Shah, sultan of Malaka, I 44.

Mahmud (Maulana Sultan) of Mesir, legendary sultan of Egypt, father of sharif Hidayat, I 277.

Ma Huan, Chinese navigator, III 216.

Mahudara, see Udara.

Mainoe (daëng), Makasar chief, IV-2 136.

Maja Agung, Majagung, Wirasaba, town, I 94, 161, 284; III 12, 34, 49; V 22, 172, 173, 269, 275; IX 37.

Majakĕrta town, district (Japan), I 164, 173, 184, 227, 277, 309, 315; II 104, 106, 107, 117; III 34, 94; IV-2 100; V 254; IX 31.

Maja Lĕgi, village, VIII 63.

Majapahit, kraton, Old Jav. kingdom, I passim; II 5-7, 57, 106, 116, 125; III 22, 25, 34, 126, 220, 274; IV-2 53, 143, 150; V 2, 8, 21, 24, 46, 56, 70, 79, 90, 151, 155, 172, 240, 242, 246; VI 290, 291, 301, 309; VII 14, 21, 22, 24, 26; VIII 11, 14, 59, 148; IX 2, 3, 5-12, 14-18, 20, 83, 87.

Maja Sanga, village, VIII 62, 63, 67, 70, 71, 84.

Maja Warna, village (mission), I 57; VI 288.

Majéné, district, South Celebes, IV-2 63.

Makam Aji, cemetery of sult. Pajang, Butuh, I 217; II 89, 100.

Makasar, town, kingdom, South Celebes, Makasarese, I 8, 80, 152, 201, 218,
254, 260, 289; II 61, 94, 95; III 21, 56, 62, 94, 184, 187, 190, 225, 228, 262, 275, 281, 282; IV-1 6, 19, 37, 45, 51, 59, 66-73, 95, 98, 100, 104, 105, 111, 120, 121, 128, 129, 132, 140, 143, 156, 165, 176, 182-186, 208; IV-2 36, 39, 61-76, 80-82, 84-89, 92-114, 116-125, 133-137, 142, 146, 150-152, 163, 165, 171-174, 178, 180, 198; V 5-8, 17, 21-24, 28, 36, 38, 41, 44, 47, 49-51, 54, 55, 57, 61, 63, 69, 72, 78, 79, 81, 83, 84, 96, 97, 100, 101, 105, 109, 110, 116, 120, 122, 129, 130, 134, 136, 143, 146, 149, 154, 157, 159, 161, 162, 169, 170, 175, 176, 181, 188-190, 192, 194-198, 201, 203, 204, 208, 213, 216, 218, 219, 232, 233, 235-238, 240, 241, 252, 254-258, 263, 265, 273; VI 275-286, 294, 299, 305; VII 1, 15, 17, 22, 27, 29, 32, 34, 42; VIII 9, 11, 12, 30, 31, 33, 35, 50, 55, 59, 111, 112, 117, 133, 137, 155, 161; IX 58-60, 62, 63, 68-72, 77-79, 82, 83, 87, 88, 94, 95.

Makdum (sèh), sent to Pasir by sult. Demak, I 42, 62.

Makdum Ibrahim (pg.), name of sunan Bonang, I 48.

Makdum Sampang, imām of the mosque of Demak, I 49, 50.

Makhdar Ibrahim (Maulana), of Gujarat, legendary father of Fadhillah, I 277.

Makinci(ng) (daëng), Makasar chief, IV-2 120.

"Malabagadadi", skipper from Gujarat, III 179.

Malabar, in South India, I 248; IV-1 176; V 6.

Malaka, town, kingdom, I 1, 14, 23, 43-47, 60, 76, 78, 79, 81, 82, 101, 103, 105, 111, 123, 124, 139-143, 149, 190, 195, 202, 203, 226, 238, 251, 270, 272, 273, 300, 301, 318; II 30, 33-35, 68, 98; III 18-20, 67, 69-71, 73, 119, 146, 164-167, 170, 171, 191, 223, 225, 227-230, 232, 246, 272, 276; IV-1 58, 77, 117, 196; V 31, 36, 56; IX 5, 7, 11, 19, 27, 29, 43, 44, 46, 50, 58, 60.

Malan (encik), Malay, V 258.

Malang, town, district, I 8, 58, 145, 164, 166, 168, 264; III 28, 29, 31, 263; IV-2 53; V 66, 213, 248, 250, 254;

69, 71, 72, 74-77, 85, 86, 88, 98, 110, 113, 135.

Manggappa (daëng), Makasar chief, IV-2 74-77; IX 68.

Mangku Bumi (pg.), brother of Sénapati Mataram, I 233; II 109, 112, 122, 128; III 3, 28, 29, 31, 33, 39.

Mangku Bumi (pg.), under sult. Agung, IV-2 9.

Mangku Bumi (pg.), name of sult. Aměngku Buwana I of Yogyakarta, II 51.

Mangku Bumi (dip.), Wira Truna, patih of png. Pugĕr, V 12, 63, 105.

Mangku Bumi (rd. ad.), name of Sura Pati, VIII 136.

Mangku Dirja, lurah, III 10.

Mangku Nagara, title of crownprince, II 129.

Mangku Nagara VII, of Surakarta, II 22.

Mangku Praja (ad.), patih jĕro under Paku Buwana I, V 240.

Mangku Rat, patih of Demak, I 66.

Mangku Rat, name of kings of Mataram, I 72, 231, 249.

Mangku Rat I (sunan), Séda Tĕgal Wangi, 1645-1677, II 75, 114; III 24, 111, 115, 141, 155, 211, 212, 241, 247, 258, 280; IV-1 1, 6-8, 22, 114, 157, 207; IV-2 4, 6, 15, 17, 27-29, 31, 41, 42, 44, 48, 139, 188, 190, 193; V 1, 2, 79; VI 289; VII 1, 3-6, 9, 13, 23, 24, 50; IX 45, 47, 48, 53-62, 65-67, 69, 70, 72-74, 86-91, 94, 95.

Mangku Rat II (sunan Amral), Karta Sura, 1677-1703, I 32, 85, 219, 252, 259, 281, 293; II 12, 52, 59, 75; III 15, 114, 209, 212, 221, 249; IV-1 2, 7, 8; IV-2 1, 3, 6, 48-50, 144, 181, 182, 186, 188, 191, 193; V 3, 10, 13, 15, 16, 18, 28, 32, 49, 58-61, 63, 64, 70, 93, 94, 105, 138, 175, 187, 201, 228, 248; VI 273, 285, 287, 306; VII 2, 4, 7, 13, 15, 18, 23-27, 32, 34, 37, 39, 40, 42, 47, 49, 50, 52, 54; VIII 10-12, 14, 18-20, 43, 63, 141, 143, 145, 148, 161, 164; IX 66, 76-80, 83, 86, 88, 91, 94, 95, 99-103.

Mangku Rat III (sunan Mas), 1703-'08, I 30, 31; II 59; III 15; IV-2 3; V 63, 113; IX 101, 103.

Mangku Rat IV (sunan Jawa), 1719- 1727, II 76, 101; III 23, 104, 124, 125.

Mangku Rat Agung, sunan Mangku Rat I, IV-1 9.

Mangku Rat (ratu), queen-consort of Mangku Rat II, VIII 18, 44, 66.

Mangku Yuda (tg.), Mad. rebel, commander, IV-2 120, 129, 181-183, 185, 187; V 9, 23, 71, 105, 178, 187; VI 288, 300, 301; VII 18, 19, 21, 26, 35, 36.

Mangku Yuda of Kĕdu, commander, V 28, 68, 116, 120, 121, 126, 175, 176, 177, 183, 185, 187, 194, 201, 212, 217, 218, 229, 231, 241.

Mangku Yuda of Panaraga, dem. Kamplang, partisan of Truna Jaya, V 132.

Mangku Yuda, Bal. commander under Mangku Rat II, VIII 31, 40, 95.

Mangopo (daëng), corporal, V 96.

Mangun Jaya, bupati under ad. Pragola of Paṭi, III 138, 140.

Mangun Jaya (ky. dem.), mantri under Mangku Rat II, VIII 24.

Mangun Jaya, of Surabaya, father of Rara Oyi, the favourite of Mangku Rat I, IV-2 3, 23.

Mangun Jaya (ky. ad.), patih of Bantĕn, IV-2 76.

Mangun Jaya (ng.), Chinese commander under Truna Jaya, V 204, 220.

Mangun Nagara (ky.), of Surabaya, IV-2 175.

Mangun Nagara (tg.), courtier, commander under Mangku Rat I, IV-2 115, 140, 164.

Mangun Onĕng (tg.), commander under sult. Agung, III 94, 95, 97, 98, 117, 118, 139, 141.

Mangun Onĕng (tg.), bupati of Paṭi under Mangku Rat II, III 143; V 14, 24, 29, 67, 71, 112, 128, 153, 175, 177, 180, 181, 183, 185, 201-203, 212, 214, 217, 218, 229, 253, 261; VI 282; VII 5.

Mangusboom, ship, V 257.

Mangun Tapa (rd.) of Madyun, commander, V 250, 267.

Manila (nyahi geḍé), wife of sunan Ngampèl Denta, I 282.

Manilla, capital of the Philippines, I 278; III 224; IV-1 120, 121.

Manipa, island, VI 288.

Mĕsir, Egypt, I 254, 263, 266, 277; II 130; V 38, 50.

Mĕsir, in Banyumas, residence of Namrud, see also Masir, Pasir, I 254; VII 32, 35, 42, 44; VIII 12; IX 88, 89.

Mĕsir (dipati), bupati of Paṭi, I 263.

Mĕsjid, see Masjid.

Michielsen (Evert), merchant, IV-1 19, 44, 45, 59, 65, 67, 72, 107, 112-114, 118, 124, 126, 127, 129-131, 134, 136, 137, 139-142; IV-2 5, 8, 9, 11.

Michielsen (Jochem), lieut., IV-2 177.

Middelburg, town (soldier), III 237; V 52, 165, 198.

"Miendil" (mas), pg. Mĕmĕnang, see also Mendil, VII 38.

miḥrab, in mosque, niche, direction of Mecca, I 35, 97, 98, 265, 271.

"Mijah" (ki), ki Jamiyah, envoy, IV-1 40.

mijil, name of metre, Jav. prosody, I 268.

Minangkabau, see Mĕnangkabau.

Mindi (mas), son of Santa Mârta, envoy, see also Mĕndi, IV-2 174.

Ming, Chinese dynasty, I 2.

Miran (Hendr.), lieut., V 99.

Mirma Gati (ky.), merchant, harbourmaster of Japara, IV-1 162, 163, 165, 170, 182, 184, 200, 202, 204-206; IV-2 90, 107, 113, 119, 131, 142, 144, 152-156, 161.

Mission, R. C., I 189, 190.

Mlambang, village, fortification, VII 23, 34-36, 38; IX 88, 89.

Mlanting (dèwi), rice goddess, Bali, I 248.

Mlaya (rd. demang), see Mĕlaya.

Mocha, port, I 278.

Modin Tuban, legendary man of religion, blacksmith, I 283.

"Moechoel", Mongolia (?), I 37, 38.

Moens (J. L.), author, I 262.

Moerstoffels (Dirck), prisoner of war, III 233, 235.

"Mogael", Mongolia, I 39.

"Mogat Sari" (rd.), governor of Pamekasan, see also Mugat Sari, IV-2 56.

Mohammed, see Muhammad.

Mohammed Usman, of Kajoran, author, IV-2 43; VII 8.

molana, see maolana.

Moloko (pulo), see Moluccas.

Moloko (nyahi gedé), daughter of sunan Ngampèl Dĕnta, I 153.

Moluccas, "Grote Oost", I 9, 11, 19, 24, 34, 45, 55, 100, 139, 148, 152, 153, 189, 289; II 35-37; III 18, 24, 53, 67, 208; IV-1 68, 77, 117, 119; IV-2 147; V 5, 6, 13, 35-37, 51, 52, 57, 272; VIII 112, 113; IX 15, 27, 46, 50.

Momu (daèng), Makasar chief, IV-2 136.

Mong Jaya (kyahi), envoy, IV-1 45.

Mongolia, I 38, 130, 175.

Montuli (kare), Mak. lieut., V 79, 84, 96, 99, 101, 149, 236, 240.

Moor, Moorish, see Muslim.

Moor (Kapitein), the governor general, IV-1 59, 131, 146, 147, 186, 189; IV-2 146.

Moortkuyl, locality near Batavia, III 252.

Moot (Aert Pleunen), shipwright, IV-1 88.

"Moro (Mamuro, Moron)", village in Surakarta, V 126, 128.

"Morob" (paté), ruler of Rembang, I 44.

moslim, see muslim.

mosque, see also masjid, I 26, 29, 99, 195, 248, 268; III 103, 113-116, 123.

mosque of Ampèl (Ngampel Dĕnta) in Surabaya, I 27, 159; VIII 19.

mosque of Cĕrbon, Cipta Rasa, I 114, 276.

mosque of Dĕmak, I 28, 30-33, 41-43, 47-51, 54, 63, 67, 70, 75, 78, 85, 92-95, 113, 114, 133, 134, 212, 228, 234, 247, 248, 256, 267, 301, 305, 308, 316; III 24, 29; VIII 121, 125, 142; IX 6-10, 89, 99.

mosque of Gumĕna, Grĕsik, I 146, 147.

mosque of Japara, V 82/83.

mosque of Kaḍiri, V 245.

mosque of Kudus, I 97, 99, 100, 148, 265; V 84.

mosque of Palembang, I 205.

mosque of Pamantingan, I 271; IX 27.

mosque of Singkal (Kaḍiri), I 59; V 251.

mosque of Sumĕnĕp, I 178.

mosque of Surabaya, see Ampèl.

mosque of Sura-Natan, Surakarta, Yogyakarta, I 268.

mosque of Tembayat, VII 38.

mosque of Tuban, I 135.

N

Nis, see Ngĕnis.
Niti Nĕgara (tg.), patih of Mangku Rat I, IV-1 20, 21; IV-2 25.
Niti Praja (ky.), treasurer of Mangku Rat I, IV-1 21; IV-2 79.
Niti Praja, mantri, guide (Hurdt), V 83, 200.
Niti Sastra (ky.), treasurer of Mangku Rat I, IV-1 21; IV-2 79, 94.
Niti Sruti, Jav. moralistic poem, I 216, 217, 309.
Niti Yuda (ky. ng.), chief of Batang, IV-1 126.
Niti Yuda (tg.), commander under Mangku Rat II, V 120, 121, 156.
Nitik Sultan Agung, legendary history, I 313.
"Njaykabawang" (pg.), ruler of Japara, II 36.
Nolpé (Jac.), captain, IV-1 55.
Noorduyn (J.), orientalist, I 126, 128, 209, 279, 280, 284, 304, 309; V 155.

Noordwijk, ship, V 272.
Noort (Olivier v.), navigator, I 151; II 60; III 205.
Norden, town (soldier), V 212.
Noronha (Michel de), count de Linhares, viceroy of Goa, III 169, 171, 223, 225, 226.
nujum (Arab.), divination, VI 299.
Numbak Anyar, company of soldiers, IV-2 99.
Numbak Cĕmĕng, company of spearmen, II 112.
Nurullah (Sèh), sunan Gunung Jati of Cĕrbon, I 49-51, 56, 95, 112-114, 118, 251, 277; IX 12.
Nusa Kambangan, island, South Coast, III 11.
Nusa Nivel, locality, Moluccas, V 96, 254.
Nusatapi, Moluccas, IV-1 119.
Nyampo, legendary man of religion, Suku Ḍomas, I 245.

O

Ocean (Indian), see Southern Ocean.
Ockersen (O.), shabandar, harbour-master, IV-1 6; IV-2 125.
Ockersz. (Corn.), merchant, IV-1 55-58.
Oei Ping Ko, Chinese captain, Japara, VIII 29.
Ombak, village, III 46.
"Ommelanden", district surrounding Batavia/Jakarta, I 7; III 252.
Onda Kara (ky.), see Anda Kara.
Onderop, sergeant, IV-2 95.
"Ondoe", village, VII 44.
Ono or *Ona* (?), (kare), messenger, South Celebes, V 273, 274.
Onrust, island in the bay of Batavia, III 62, 190, 269; IV-1 88.
Oortman (Jan), soldier, V 105.
Ongguq (pg.), ruler of West Madura, I 171, 172.
"Oost", Grote-, Great East, see Moluccas.

Oostende, port (soldier), V 115.
Oosterwijck (Jan), senior merchant, III 185, 255.
"Oosthoek", see Eastern Corner (of Java).
"Oost-Indië", see Indonesia.
"Oost-Indiën (Oud- en Nieuw-)", book by F. Valentijn, I 152, 153, 289; IX 82.
Opak, river, Mataram, I 7, 206, 220, 222, 223, 311, 313; II 49, 51, 76, 83, 84; III 110, 111; IV-1 10, 14; VII 36, 39, 43; IX 21, 22, 28.
Oppijnen (J. v.), captain, IV-2 163, 166, 174.
Oppolzer, astronomer, II 129.
orang kaya (Malay), member of the aristocracy, III 106, 117, 118, 136, 195, 206; IV-1 109, 112; IV-2 66, 127.

P

116, 120, 121, 131, 224, 250, 255;
VII 3, 8, 24, 28, 33, 37-39, 41, 46;
VIII 89; IX 8-10, 12-15, 17, 18, 20-
22, 26-33, 37, 38, 55, 77-79, 83, 86-
89, 94.

Pajang (sultan), Jaka Tingkir, I 297;
II 85.

Pajang (ad.), ruler under suzerainty of
Mataram, rd. Sida Wini, II 99, 100;
III 4, 36, 44-47.

Pajang (ad.), pg. Gagak-Baning, brother
of Sénapati Mataram, II 99, 100.

Pajang (pg. tg.), son of sult. Agung, rd.
mas Sahwawrat, IV-1 6.

Pajang, village in Madyun, V 154.

Pajangkungan, territory of tg. Paṭi, IV-1
112, 187.

Pajarakan, port in East Java, I 179, 187,
189, 194, 195, 297; IV-2 87-89, 108;
V 24, 151; IX 18, 69.

Pajarakan (ng.), bupati, IV-2 89.

Pajatèn, village, IV-1 147.

Pa'juma or *Pajumang* (aru), Mak. chief,
V 270.

Pakacangan, district in Madura, I 164;
III 84, 89.

Pakalongan, seaport, town, district, I
272; III 120, 179, 180, 182, 199, 228,
247, 266; IV-1 19, 126, 177; IV-2
109, 133, 144, 145, 149; V 11, 12,
78; VII 14, 16, 26, 45; VIII 13, 47;
IX 76, 90.

Pa'Kamar, author, I 293.

Pakaway, lieut., VI 299.

Pakis, village in Grobogan, II 7.

Pakis (nyahi ag.), daughter of ki Gĕtas
Pandawa, II 5-7.

Pakis Dadu (nyahi geḍé), daugther of ki
geḍé Séséla, II 5, 6.

Pakis Wiring, village, IV-2 144, 145.

Paku (rd.), name of prabu Satmata,
sunan Giri, I 140, 142, 285, 286; II
60.

Pakuan, see Pakuwan, II 35.

Paku Buwana, royal name, Mataram
dynasty, I 72.

Paku Buwana I, sunan (Puger), Kartasura, 1703-'19, I 131, 280; II 59; III
248; IV-2 41, 44; V 10, 63, 67, 94,
240; VII 10; VIII 131, 164, 166,
167; IX 80, 101, 103.

Paku Buwana II, sunan, Surakarta,
1726-'49, II 20.

Paku Buwana III, sunan, Surakarta,
1749-'83, I 95, 265; II 50; III 155,
268.

Paku Buwana VII, sunan, Surakarta,
1830-'58, I 291; II 50.

Pakuncèn, village, II 117.

Pakung Wati, kraton, Cĕrbon, I 275.

Pakurang, Madu Rĕtna, Truna Jaya's
kraton in Madura, IV-2 60, 176.

Pakuwan Pajajaran, kingdom, West Java,
I 106, 115, 117-119, 121-123, 253,
277, 279; II 35; IX 12, 13.

Palabuhan, riverport, river Brantas, III
31; V 45, 155, 160, 168, 217, 269.

Palabuhan (mas), of Pasuruhan, ratu
Wétan, wife of Mangku Rat I, mother
of png. Pugĕr and png. Singasari, IV-2
31; VII 4.

Pala Dadi, Raja Dadi, village, west of
Wirasaba, III 33.

Palaka (raja or aru), Buginese king, V
146, 189, 190, 193, 194, 200, 254,
257; VI 276, 282, 283, 285-287, 290,
300; IX 83.

Palakaran, royal residence, Madura, I
171; III 87.

Palakaran (pg.), Pragalba or pg.
Ongguq, ruler of Madura, I 171, 172.

"*Palanangka*", Pangkalan Tangka, cemetery, Banten, I 82.

Palang, village, V 66.

Palar, village (Klaṭèn), II 13; IV-2 17.

Palémbang, town, district, kingdom, see
also Tulembang, I 37-40, 44, 46, 62,
83, 95, 122, 124, 125, 128, 129, 159,
166, 167, 199-205, 279, 300-303; II
55, 65-67; III 18, 19, 37, 40, 51, 53-
66, 69, 70, 73, 108, 128, 132, 133,
137-140, 148, 156, 157, 167, 174, 185,
186, 208; IV-2 184; V 3, 36, 57;
VIII 59; IX 7, 8, 13, 19, 20, 29, 50,
56, 57, 60, 62.

Palémbang (ki mas), name of png.
Tranggana of Demak, I 36, 40, 47,
301.

Palémbang anom (pg.), molana arya
Sumangsang of Demak, I 36.

Palémbang (sunan), man of religion, I
301.

"*Pallandinge*", village, IV-2 113.

Palmer van den Broek (W.), author, I
293; II 58; III 83.

Pal Putih, Tugu, Yogyakarta, II 121.

Q

R

S

Suta Gati, spy, V 149.
Suta Jaya (ky. mas), Javanese clerk, employed by Couper, IV-2 157.
Suta Jaya, guardsman, IV-2 93.
Suta Karti, lurah, horse expert, IV-1 122.
Suta Karti, Kalang chief, partisan of Truna Jaya, V 221.
Suta Krama, umbul of Surabaya, V 80, 129.
Suta Menggala (rd.), of Pana Raga, V 145.
Sutana, Mal. skipper, IV-2 88.
Suta Nanga (kentol), son of ng. Wira Dikara, IV-1 181-183, 185, 187.
Suta Nangdita, envoy, IV-2 35.
Suta Naya (ng.), patih of Pana Raga, V 145.
Sutantaka, messenger, V 145, 153.
Suta Pati, advisor of rd. Truna Jaya, V 253.
Suta Patra, messenger, V 152.
Suta Praja, guardsman, IV-2 93.
Suta Prana (ky. dem.), councillor of sult. Agung, III 118.
Suta Prana (lurah), commander in Panarukan, IV-2 87, 101.
Suta Prana, rebel, V 211.

Suta Sirrebon, Jav. soldier, V 98.
Suta Truna, Jav. colonist in Bekasih, IV-1 144.
Suta Truna, son of bupati Wira Atmaka of Japara, IV-1 206.
Suta Truna, murdered by rd. Truna Jaya, IV-2 60, 177.
Suta Wangsa (lurah), envoy, IV-2 125.
Suta Wangsa, name of Mandaraka, patih of Mangku Rat II, V 65.
Suta Wangsa, man of religion, messenger, V 213.
Suta Wangsa (mas), messenger, V 143.
Suta Wijaya (rd. ng.), name of Sénapati Mataram, II 22, 23, 41, 44, 45.
Suwanda (nyahi riya), mother of png. Tanpa Nangkil, brother of sult. Agung, III 4.
Suwandana, son of tg. Bau Reksa, III 179.
Suwéla Cala, legendary king of Mĕḍang Kamulan, I 269, 310.
Swaan (W.), author, III 96.
Swanagaran, village (Prawata, Demak), I 259.
Syuh Brasta, cannon of sult. Agung, III 55, 156.

T

Tabanan, Bal. kingdom, I 198, 300; III 259, 260.
Tabanan, Bal. soldier, V 165.
Tack (François), captain, I 32; IV-2 112; V 29, 37, 39, 41-43, 45, 46, 48, 53-57, 63, 64, 66, 67, 68, 76, 87, 89, 96, 102, 104, 105, 110, 114-120, 124, 126, 128, 130, 136, 138, 142-145, 151, 154, 158-160, 163, 164, 168, 177, 178, 185-187, 199, 201, 202, 204-209, 223-225, 230-232, 234, 235, 237-241, 243, 244, 259, 268, 274; VII 28, 30, 35,
47; VIII 11, 21, 24, 25, 45-48, 55, 56, 58-73, 75-78, 81, 84-100, 103, 106, 110, 111, 117, 120, 123, 126, 135, 139, 143, 144, 153, 154, 159, 160, 162, 167; IX 79, 93, 94, 96-98, 102, 103.
"Tagaril", sunan Gunung Jati, I 50, 112, 276, 277; V 261; IX 11.
Taiwan, Formosa, IV-1 119.
Tajem, female servant, IV-1 28.
Taji, toll-gate of Mataram (East), I 217, 222, 309; II 49-51, 121; III 65, 69.

119, 123, 125, 133-138, 140-143, 145-153, 156, 158, 159, 161-179, 181, 183, 184, 187, 191, 192; V 4-7, 9, 14, 21-24, 27, 29, 32, 43, 46, 48, 49, 51, 54, 59, 61, 64, 67, 70-72, 98, 101, 105, 110, 116, 129, 130, 133, 142, 143, 145, 150, 151, 153, 155-157, 161, 169, 178, 179, 181, 182, 184, 187, 189, 191, 194, 213, 217, 220, 227, 228, 230, 232, 233, 239-241, 243, 245, 247-250, 252-255, 267, 270; VI, VII passim; VIII 9-12, 20, 22, 48-50, 112; IX 46, 67-73, 76-83, 86-89, 94, 96, 101.

Truna Jaya (gunung), mountain, East Java, VI 308, 309.

Trusan, village, see Tĕrusan.

"*Tsi attap*", see Ci Atap.

"*Tsi ompo*", see Ci Ompo.

Tuanku Rao, book by Parlindungan, I 18, 276.

Tuban, seaport, district, kingdom, I 8, 27, 48, 49, 54, 57, 69, 87, 90, 93, 96, 101, 114, 127, 130-136, 142, 144, 147, 148, 150, 151, 157, 160-162, 164, 171, 180, 185, 215, 217, 230, 231, 240, 262, 263, 269, 270, 273, 281-284, 286-288, 290, 313, 316; II 58, 62, 67, 78, 85, 123-125, 132; III 18, 30-34, 38, 41, 42, 44, 47-52, 77, 78, 135, 208, 216, 279, 289; IV-1 82, 177, 181, 194; IV-2 9, 32, 89, 93, 118, 123-125, 173, 182; V 254; IX 10, 14, 22, 32, 33, 38, 39, 50, 96.

Tuban (ad. or tg.), rulers, I 48, 133; II 77, 78, 82, 83, 86, 91; III 36, 37; V 77, 129, 146, 148, 164, 188, 190, 196, 201, 232, 233, 239; VII 18; VIII 9, 19, 57.

Tuban (modin), man of religion, legendary blacksmith, I 283.

Tuban (perdana pati), Ambonese ruler, I 253.

Tuban Besi (perdana), chief of Hitu, II 37.

Tudunan, Tudunang, (kali), river Sé-rang, Central Java, see also Teḍunan, V 85, 86, 97, 102, 108, 111, 114/5.

Tugu Mengangkang, legendary border (mounts Sumbing and Sendara), I 42.

Tujan (kare), Mak. sergeant, V 99.

Tulang Bawang, district, South Sumatra, III 275; IV-1 40.

Tulémbang, town, see Palembang, I 200, 301.

Tulèn, legendary country, I 20.

Tulolo (daèng), Mak. leader, IV-2 84-86.

Tumapĕl, Singasari, Old Jav. kraton, I 179, 189, 293, 294.

Tumapĕl (dip. mas), nephew of panem-bahan Agung of Giri, commander in Surabaya, V 13, 45, 49, 65, 69, 129, 169, 189, 192, 194, 196, 217, 229, 231, 232, 238, 247, 249, 256, 275; IX 76, 79.

tumenggung, title of military commanders.

Tumenggung (raja), ruler of Palembang, III 276.

Tumenggung (rd.), son of Wayahan Pa-madekan of Tabanan, Bali, III 260.

Tumenggung Mataram, title of grand-viziers, see also patih, IV-1 14; IX 35.

Tunggul Pĕtung, mythical king, I 222.

Tunggul Wulung, mythical fish, olor, river Ompak (Sénapati Mataram), II 76.

Tunglur (Tonglor), village, fortress, V 43, 146, 149, 151, 152, 154, 156, 157, 164, 240, 268.

Tuntang, river, I 66; VIII 157.

"*Tu Ragam*", (ky.), "highpriest", (Ab-dur-Rahman?), pangulu under Mang-ku Rat I, IV-2 153.

Turkey, Turks, I 51, 76, 113, 273; III 99, 119.

Tuuk (H. Neubronner van der), orien-talist, I 285, 296.

Tuwan di Bitay, theologian, Acheh, I 266.

U

V

W

Wangsa Menggala (ki), son of Wangsa Dipa, IV-2 130, 154.

Wangsa Menggala (ky.), Jav. rebel, V 220.

Wangsa Naka, servant of Jayeng Pati, IV-2 177.

Wangsa Nanga (rd.), envoy, IV-1 174.

Wangsa Nata (ng.), Balinese commander in Kartasura, VIII 31, 40, 65, 66, 68, 70, 76-80, 82, 86, 89, 90, 93, 95.

Wangsa Naya, lurah from Japara, V 138.

Wangsa Naya (ky.), soldier, VIII 137.

Wangsantaka, author, see also Wangsa Antaka, IV-2 56.

Wangsa Pada (si), envoy, IV-1 94.

Wangsa Pati, envoy, IV-2 65, 120, 127.

Wangsa Patra, messenger, IV-1 174; IV-2 190.

Wangsa Praja, umbul of Jěnu (Tuban), IV-1 195.

Wangsa Prana (ng.), umbul, steward in Japara, IV-1 194, 205; IV-2 119, 120, 130-132, 173, 174.

Wangsa Prana, bupati of Surabaya, V 13.

Wangsa Raja (ng.), bupati of Semarang, III 280; IV-1 19, 67, 91, 103, 108-110, 113, 117, 125, 130, 131, 140, 143.

Wangsa Suta (si), envoy, IV-2 35.

Wangsa Taka, shabandar of Juwana, see also Wangsa Antaka, Wangsantaka, IV-1 122.

Wangsa Truna, mantri jěro, IV-2 23.

Wangsèng Gati (arya), Mad. commander, IV-2 141, 182, 184, 185, 187; V 29, 71, 91, 97, 112, 194, 250, 264, 267; VII 19, 30.

Wangsèng Rana, rebel, pirate in Madura, VIII 48-50, 53, 54; IX 96.

Wapen van Amsterdam, ship, III 68.

Wapen van Delft, ship, III 223.

Wardi (S.), author, I 31, 33, 280.

Wareng, Bareng, village, IV-2 30.

Warga, Sripada, spy, III 71, 102, 150, 160, 173, 174, 183, 189, 242.

Warga Dalem (mas), local chief, commander under Mangku Rat II, V 213, 250, 259.

Warga Utama, ruler of Wirasaba, Banyumas, II 65.

waring, texture of plaited fibres or straw, flag of Wana Kusuma rebels, VII 47; VIII 15.

waringin kurung, fenced banyan trees on the alun-alun, II 8, 70; III 10, 14, 106, 122, 209, 290; see also Wringin.

"Warsa Denti" of "Yayana" (Cahyana), Banyumas, VIII 41.

Waru, village, district (Blora), V 66.

Waruk Tengah or *Kalang,* village, V 142.

Warung, Warong, district, Blora, I 228; II 107, 108; IV-2 138, 182; V 110, 125; VII 18; IX 32.

Warwijck (Wijbr. v.), vice-admiral, I 135; III 19.

Waston (Humphrey), merchant, III 267.

Wasya (raja), chief from South Celebes, IV-2 88.

"Waterkasteel", Taman Sari, park belonging to the kraton of Yogyakarta, III 110; VIII 63.

"Waterpoort", gate of the Castle of Batavia, IV-2 147.

Wates, "Watas", village, district, IV-1 144; V 18-20, 27, 28, 30, 31, 38, 67, 90, 111, 115, 116, 125, 131, 138, 249; VII 31, 33, 44; VIII 39.

Watu Aji (ky.), legendary ancestor, Ngrombé, I 59.

Watu Takan, village, V 142.

Watu Tinap, village, V 117, 118.

Wawala, village, IV-2 21.

Wayah (ki), father of ratu Malang, IV-2 15-17.

Wayahan Indissan, Balinese soldier, V 165.

Wayahan Pamaděkan (Ngurah), of Tabanan, Bali, I 300; III 259, 260.

wayang, Jav. puppet theatre, I 70, 71, 247, 258, 267, 295, 306, 307; III 203.

wayang bèbèr, scrolls, I 211, 258, 306; II 16; III 24.

wayang krèbèt, wayang bèbèr, II 16.

wayang krucil, flat wooden puppets, III 213.

wayang kulit, leather puppets, III 24, 105.

wayang purwa, leather puppets, III 23, 213.

Wědi, village, district, I 62, 211, 230, 315; II 121-123; III 199, 200; IX 45.

Weesick (Arent v.), prisoner of war, III 7.

Weesp, redoubt of Batavia, III 151.

X, Y, Z

Printed in the United States
By Bookmasters